The
Abolition
of
Poverty

The
Abolition
of
Poverty

DAVID HOROWITZ

PRAEGER PUBLISHERS
New York · Washington · London

PRAEGER PUBLISHERS
111 Fourth Avenue, New York, N.Y. 10003
5, Cromwell Place, London S.W.7, England

Published in the United States of America in 1969
by Praeger Publishers, Inc.

© 1969 by Praeger Publishers, Inc.

Library of Congress Catalog Card Number: 71–87826

Printed in the United States of America

Contents

Preface

This book deals with the most crucial problem of the twentieth century: the existence of poverty in the midst of plenty. The widening gap between the standards of living of the developed and the underdeveloped nations, the clash and conflict in the cities of some of the affluent nations, and the tragic implications of both of these situations for the peace of the world provide the motivation for an analysis of ways to eliminate poverty once and for all.

Discussions at the annual meeting of the board of governors of the World Bank, of which I have been a member for the past fifteen years, and UNCTAD conferences have stimulated my interest in the solution to this pressing problem. I am convinced that the technological and economic prerequisites for wiping out this age-old scourge of mankind are now in existence. My personal experience in development work in Israel has confirmed me in this belief. Thus, the aim of this book is to explore the whole range of the problems of poverty and to describe the interaction and interdependence of policies designed to abolish it in developed and in underdeveloped nations.

The principal means to rid man of poverty—population control, encouragement of the so-called green revolution in agriculture, and industrialization—will all conduce to a structural transformation of the world's economy and, through large-scale investment, to a global shift to the secondary and tertiary stages of production. But a major, though not the only, constraint on economic development that has the abolition of poverty as its end is shortage of capital for investment in underdeveloped nations. The traditional sources of such capital, grants and private investment, are limited and stagnant, and new sources must be tapped. One of these is the free capital market, to which the underdeveloped nations have presently little, if any, access. The search for hitherto unexploited methods that will allow poor nations to profit from financing by the immense and ever expanding capital market has led me to formulate a plan to mobilize capital for underdeveloped nations.

The success of all efforts to abolish poverty depends on the mobility of capital and other resources, such as skill and technology, and on appropriate political action. I think it is necessary for political leaders, economists, sociologists, and others involved in the work to end poverty to look to the horizons opened up by modern technology and economics, to define thoroughly the objectives of development, and to propose the methods to be applied to meet those objectives. The cooperative ordering of the world's economic machinery can bring about the abolition of poverty.

DAVID HOROWITZ

The
Abolition
of
Poverty

Introduction: Purposive Economics

Poverty, the scourge of man from time immemorial, is, in our age of modern technology and new economics, a superfluous and preventable affliction. It has ceased to be the remorseless and inescapable subject of mysterious and ungovernable forces. By conscious human effort and control it can be abolished as a function of global economic policy.

The economic disparity between classes in the developed countries is narrowing, that between the developed and underdeveloped nations is widening. Elimination of poverty as a normal socio-economic phenomenon depends on interaction and interrelation of the developed industrialized and the underdeveloped parts of the world and on the continuation of the social policy presently conducted in the developed parts, culminating in guaranteed minimum incomes, full employment, and greater control of cyclical crises.

The reactions to the Great Depression of the 1930's in the countries of the West differed extremely in terms of the philosophical and social ideologies they generated or reinforced, but they had one common denominator in economics: the tendency toward a guided economy. The New Deal in America and the welfare state emerging from the slump in Britain represented a reaction to the economic crisis of the interwar period and had one common denominator: economic management in the spirit of Keynesian economics. The intellectual conception of this period was firmly anchored to an ideology that rejected the autonomism of economic forces as the *ultima ratio* of economic science and scouted the grim and gloomy prospect of the exclusive functioning of an economic mechanism, with its corollary of foreordained misery and decline. The relationship between investment, employment, flow of money, and economic activity could be governed and directed toward certain social and economic objectives by a conscious policy. This is the credo of the new thinking.

The assumption, therefore, is that the volume of effective demand and investment and the utilization of resources should no longer be the resultant of a parallelogram of economic forces with a self-controlling and self-propelled autonomous machinery but should be subjected more and more to the interplay of conscious human policy within the national and the international economy. These currents, speeded by the despair that was bred in the Great Depression and the collapse of the gold standard, swelled the power and intensified the push of economic direction. Economic guidance had its climax, by force of events, in the managed economy of the Second World War.

The basis of the new socio-economic conception was the emergence of economics as a discipline based on exact thinking and capable of influencing the chain of events in society by application of conscious policies formed by rational analysis and pointed toward normative goals. The successful application of anticyclical policies, the birth of the welfare state, and—most important—the demonstration of economic growth combined with full employment and comparative stability, and the narrowing of economic gaps between social classes thanks to a deliberate redistribution of national income— these socio-economic processes opened up new vistas of advance and injected a new and non-Utopian dose of humanism into economic policy and practice.

The postwar period amply proved the virtue of a guided economy of full employment and growth, with few and moderate recessions and some containment of inflationary pressures in the developed world. Economics ceased to be a "dismal science." The dark prophecies of the classical theory, with a nadir of hopelessness, did not come true. The specter of human misery and of its inexorability is being laid to rest. The new economic activism asserts a power and prestige unconfined to a forecast of economic developments and capable, in the last resort, of shaping socio-economic events.

Central banks, once the bulwark of the "dismal science" and defenders of the automatic readjustments of an autonomous economic mechanism, give up their old and antiquated attitudes and, by conducting anticyclical policies, are integrated into the mosaic of modern economics. They no longer limit their policies to response to market incentives, but, invoking the idea of a flexible equilibrium, are transformed into the powerful instrument of a guided, managed, and directed economy.

The progress of analysis in applied economics facilitates the evaluation of different courses in the economic organism and the prediction, with a fairly high degree of exactness, of the results of alternative actions. No more are economic forecasts the function of vague guesswork. The components of the most intricate economic pattern become measurable. Not only is the pace of economic activity quantitatively determined, but it is influenced by a series of accelerators and brakes with a view to promoting balanced growth.

The control panel of a national economy is equipped with a set of switches, buttons, and levers by which economic factors can be activated or arrested, reinforced or weakened. The interaction and interdependence of such instruments are the essence of economic and social engineering. Man and society are being emancipated from the hegemony of gigantic, latent, mysterious, and seemingly sinister forces. The fear that an unexpected combination of them could bring the world economy once again to the brink of a devastating crisis similar in magnitude and depth to that of the Great Depression and its protracted aftermath is gradually receding. The set of instruments of economic policy, guided by the control panel, and the know-how to apply them are ready for operation.

At the same time, with the diminishing danger of our becoming the victims of hidden, unknown, and awesome economic forces, the probability of a failure of the economic and social organism because of the shortcomings of those who handle the control panel and its instruments increases. The set of switches that direct and guide the economic mechanism is complicated and intricate. The slightest mistake in handling the main wheel may mean a convulsion resembling upheavals generated in the past by blind economic forces, though less formidable.

The instruments, although still imperfect and unrefined, were to a great extent available in the United States in 1929, but there was no determination to use them, and knowledge of their handling was defective. The principal reason economic policy could not react effectively to the risk of crisis was a reluctance to use unorthodox remedies and stimulants that could have mitigated and shortened the crisis. Preconceived notions of what could be done by economic policy and the use of economic controls and of what is legitimate in such circumstances militated against prompt and timely intervention and, as a result, the ever deepening crisis took its disastrous course.

In the second half of the twentieth century, no such inhibitions restrain or thwart economic policy. The tools of fiscal and monetary policy are extensively and continuously employed to prevent economic polarization and excessive amplitudes of economic swings. On the other hand, in some underdeveloped countries, the instruments of economic control and guidance are at hand, but faulty manipulation of the main wheel produces inflation, recurring balance-of-payments crises, physical shortages, heavy indebtedness, and a distorted design of prices, production, and investment. In other words, the instruments are widely used but in the wrong direction. In a modern state where the instruments of monetary expansion are available it is easy to engender expansion without a corresponding flow of goods and services and thus to entail a tremendous waste and misappropriation of resources.

Economic controls are handled by men just on the borderline between economics, sociology, and politics. Man is a product of society and social forces as well as of his individual qualities and shortcomings. The very power and precision of the instruments of control become a source of slumbering and imminent hazard. The currents and cross-currents of social thinking, feeling, and reflexes and the dynamics of economic interests bear on the method, efficiency, and aim of the controls. On the one hand, skill in mastering the complex instrumentalities has improved immensely, and, on the other, the instruments themselves have become geared to human will and reason and thus more susceptible to the influence of the interests, emotions, and pressures of political and economic forces. Thus, the mechanism of nearly unknown forces with only vaguely comprehended rules of behavior is supplanted by interaction of human factors and by the parallelogram of social forces, which shapes and directs the economy. The very fact that a certain set of ideas and evaluations has penetrated man's consciousness turns this psychological event into a social and political force. The impoverishment theory (*Verelendungstheories*) so utterly disproved by developments in the twentieth century is a case in point. The assumption of growing economic and social polarization is contradicted by the narrowing of the gap between social and economic classes in the modern, highly developed, industrialized states of America and Europe. This reversal of a trend that was visible and described at the commencement of the first Industrial Revolution wrecked the doctrine of progressive and foredoomed impoverishment.

To what extent have the policies applied to that end, at least in their inception, been prompted and pursued by revulsion against the process of social polarization and impoverishment and, alike, by fear of the political and social repercussions of it?

The theoretical forecast itself set factors in motion that balked its materialization in economic and social life. The very consciousness of the problem became a powerful element, counteracting the onset of impoverishment and polarization.

The extension of economic controls lends new interest to the question of who handles the control panel and its instruments. First and foremost are the governments: their weight and influence are growing concurrently with the power and multiplication of social controls. The gross national product has risen in the United States about seventeen times, from an estimated $40.3 billion in 1913 to $785.0 billion in 1967. Total government expenditures, federal, state, and local, rose from $3 billion in 1913 to over $175 billion in 1967, over fifty-eight times. The trend is even more pronounced in Europe: it is estimated that, in highly developed countries, about one-third of the economy is government controlled. Fiscal and monetary policy programs, redistribution of national income, social welfare, and full employment had their part in determining the shape of things to come.

However, the pattern of the socio-economic chart is blurred and distorted by contradictory interests and tendencies. The men and women at the control panel must respond to the new challenge by renouncing the social and political dictates of their own authority and action if the equilibrium of an expanding economy and society and its optimum progress are to be achieved. They must behave in conformity with the long-range interests of state and society and, frequently, in conflict with the short-term, vested interests of strong pressure groups and the myopic longings of large sections of the population.

The institutional set-up that prescribes who is to handle the new and powerful controls and how is subject to an agonizing test. Those at the control panel are in duty bound to perceive the totality of currents and cross-currents, interests, social and economic components, and countervailing forces, and this overall survey must often call for action that cannot but disregard particular interests, however influential they are.

The new functions not only demand a profound understanding of complex and delicate tasks, but, simultaneously, make obligatory a release from dependence upon the social and economic forces that raised the "controllers" to their position of power and direction. This is one of the sternest challenges of modern democracy.

As the issue becomes more involved and intricate, only a very limited segment of society can fathom the labyrinth of social point and counterpoint, measure the weight of economic factors, and become familiar with the convoluted mechanism of a modern state and economy. The scientific analysis and the policy conclusions based on it cannot easily be conveyed in simple terms to an uninitiated and multitudinous agglomeration of individuals. Formidable socio-political forces can be marshalled around the irrelevant and the ephemeral, while the dominant and decisive stay obscure and are confined to the periphery.

Most detective stories have a common device, the red herring, a diversion introduced at some complicated and crucial point in the plot. In the public life of modern democracies, the red herring occupies an important place, either as a trick or as a deliberate diversion or gambit in the political game or as a result of the confusion of real, vital, and fundamental issues with what is neither germane nor consequential. Popular slogans and charismatic personalities become the red herrings in the great thriller of decision-making. "Audiences of all kinds most applaud what they like best, and in social comment, the test of audience approval, far more than the test of truth, comes to influence comment" (Galbraith).

In internal as well as in external politics, the compass of the electorate is in inverse ratio to the possibility of grasping the essential and momentous and discarding the evanescent and immaterial. It is the plain man in the street who is confronted with the issues to be decided. By predisposition and training, he resembles the naive realist of philosophy. He believes in what he sees. The naive realist, who never heard of the theory of knowledge or of the critique of pure reason, relates himself to the world through the medium of his empirical common sense, whose limitations he does not realize. But the same plain man in the street, just like the politician, is inclined to rely on his simple, unproblematic, and unquestioning logic in appraising and in responding to economic and sociological issues. However, issues become more baffling and technical with the use of highly tortuous economic controls and policies. Naive realism, deprived as it is of the more elaborate and sophisticated instruments of thinking, cannot discern their essence. Economics and sociology are subjects of great complexity, but the public called upon to adjudicate on economic and social questions is not disposed to admit this. It will decline to confess the inferiority of purely empirical and superficial impressions and seems to rely entirely on common sense, an ambition not unlike essaying to disentangle the problems of Einsteinian physics by the application of arithmetic.

In underdeveloped countries, democracy suffered many reverses in the past decade mainly because the gap between the ability to understand the problems at issue and the need for clear-cut decisions is greatest there. These shortcomings intensify the temptation to resort to totalitarian ideology and to totalitarian regimes as a short-cut to unraveling the twisted riddles of a modern state, its society, and economy.

Meanwhile, the instruments that control social and economic life are acquiring greater strength and scope. Monetary policy, central banking, fiscal policies, all serve the identical purpose of social engineering and economic management.

Technically, the control and determination of social and economic processes are easier and more effective in our time, but, humanly and socially, they become more problematic. As decision-making dependence on the socio-political mechanism is accentuated not only is understanding of the function of behavior of a number of factors imperative but the will power to meddle in their interplay becomes indispensable. We have to handle the instruments of economic analysis and performance that govern the seesaw rhythm of economic life. The man applying the necessary skills and arts is the product of a given social, political, and historical milieu. The knowledge and talent to protect the societies of mankind from hunger and privation are forthcoming, but, with them, invariably, come the motivations of individual men and women with their flaws and complexes, their sensitivity to the thrusts and drags of interest and prejudice and wisdom and illusions of a modern society.

Tales of the distressing and somber world of the early Industrial Revolution, the picture of a famished proletariat and grey, hopeless slums, of penniless masses, of accumulation of misery and malnutrition—like ghosts, these shadows of a hopeless and ghastly era still haunt the minds and conscience of twentieth-century mankind. The heart-rending descriptions of Charles Dickens and Gerhart Hauptmann and the pungent and painful analyses of Marx and Engels are embedded deep in the consciousness of modern society. They are, in a way, part of its spiritual heritage and have launched movements that reverberate strongly in the national and international affairs and in the economic and social interrelations of our days. These were movements of reaction against the realities of unplumbed misery and unspeakable poverty matched by a detachment inspired by the classical economic theory, which proclaims the iron law of wages and the inevitability of social polarization as the outcome of the normal functioning of economic laws.

The revolt against this seemingly inexorable contrast and social polarization was, in fact, a product of the same classical theory and based on its apology and apotheosis. It appeared in the guise of a scientific dogma, carefully preserving the tenets of classical economics but introducing a concept of socio-political determination. It assumed that the economic forces climaxing in the concentration of capital would find their counterpart in a concentration of social forces of mass discontent generating a mighty political movement of the proletariat, which would finally accomplish the consummation of its ideas in a social revolution transferring all means of production to the nation. Here was a new reflection of the notion of a historical, inescapable process of social and economic determinism and of the identification of a revolutionary movement with the underlying forces of history.

The Marxian rationalization of this approach chose as its point of departure three anticipations by which the whole conception stands or falls: progressive impoverishment, the rise of imperialism, and the increasing frequency and gravity of cyclical economic crises. All three have to pass the test of economic criticism. Their social and political implications are economic in essence and cause and must argue with economic reality.

The theory of impoverishment envisages a development that must result in the rich getting richer and the poor getting poorer. This surmise of a continuous deterioration in living standards was an essential link in the chain of events foreseen by Marxian doctrine. The revolutionary perspective could only materialize if the lot of the proletariat became worse and its living standards fell.

The actual development of modern society did not, however, confirm the theory: neither empirical observation nor statistical analysis verifies the prognosis of descending standards. On the contrary, welfare and prosperity, as well as social security, are more widely spread, and in modern industrialized nations living standards are rising. Marxian thinking failed to envision the profound and all-embracing metamorphosis of modern society brought about by new economic and social trends and tendencies, by technological changes, and by the redistribution of democratic power. Labor is no longer a commodity priced at the cost of its maintenance and reproduction. The conception of free labor market fluctuating in conformity with the law of demand and supply and subordinated to those fluctuations does not square with the realities of a society in which labor is highly organized in trade unions, in some cases as a mighty monopoly. Impoverishment does not eventuate. Moreover, there is ample statistical evidence that standards of living and labor are rising progressively and even spectacularly in a way never conceived by the experts of the "dismal science" and the Cassandras of penury.

The idea of polarization and impoverishment as driving forces of a revolutionary social change was doomed the moment the vicious circle of economic determinism had been broken and new vistas of better living conditions dawned. Under conditions of full employment and of the welfare state, the theory of a change produced by psychological and political repercussions of tribulation and distress could hardly offer any attraction to a political movement.

All this applies to the industrialized nations of the West. Things are entirely different in the underdeveloped countries, and the gulf between the two regions of the world is deepening day after day.

Two-thirds of humanity lives on or below subsistence level.

This is the most crucial economic problem of our time. The desire to rise above this level is a most powerful spur of ferment and expectancy. Conflict is aggravated by what is termed a revolution of rising expectations, and a crisis becomes well-nigh unavoidable.

The revolution of rising expectations is fraught with many illusions. The "paradise" of Western standards seems within easy reach; the realities of the present situation appear, with even greater verisimilitude than before, a horrendous inferno. Acquiescence in a fate of wretchedness and poverty is gone. It is true that, with modern technology and the vast accumulation of wealth in the Western industrialized world, the distance the under-developed countries must travel to reach the stage of self-perpetuating and self-sustained growth could be shortened by importing capital and skill. However, the tortuous path to development and modern standards is strewn with pitfalls and jeopardies. There is no magic short cut to welfare and high standards. Herculean effort and a lengthy and difficult period of transition are not to be escaped.

Awareness of new possibilities and impatience with present status are the basis of the revolution of rising expectations and bring about a ruinous collision. These are the problems confronting the underdeveloped world, where the trend is one of steady aggravation. But the dynamics of the trend are a matter of even greater concern than is the trend itself. Their cumulative effect is adverse and far reaching, focusing on three points: demography, income, and investment.

If present indications persist, demographic projection envisages the doubling of the population of the world at the end of the twentieth century and a fundamental shift in its composition. Today, about two-thirds of it lives in underdeveloped countries; at the close of the century, four-fifths of the world's people will live in underdeveloped countries, and one-fifth will live in developed and industrialized areas. A swing of such magnitude will have widespread repercussions.

The tendency for the GNP to rise rapidly in the developed world will be unchecked, and it is estimated that it will come to $6,000 billion in the year 2000, as opposed to $1,850 billion now, while the economic growth of the underdeveloped nations will lag far behind. A handful of people on one side will be faced by a mass of economically underdeveloped people on the other, with all the inherent economic, political, and cultural dangers that the confrontation signifies. If, today, each citizen of an industrialized country is faced by two citizens in underdeveloped countries, at the end of this century he will be faced by four underprivileged inhabitants of those countries. Thus, a relatively dwindling number of people controlling extensive productive capacity and high technology per person will be arrayed against a growing number of people fighting for their very existence under the mounting pressure of greater numbers upon restricted resources. Of course, in such a development, the absolute level of consumption and demand counts not less than do the relative magnitudes.

The gap in the growth of the real gross product between developed and underdeveloped countries will widen. In the period 1950–66, the expansion of the GNP in the underdeveloped world came to 4.5 per cent per annum, but the population explosion reduced the per capita annual increment to no more than 2 per cent, while in the developed countries of the West the overall rise in the GNP was 5 per cent per annum and 3.6 per cent per capita. By the end of this century, the gap will have increased enormously.

This climbing of the per capita GNP must be viewed in its absolute terms if it is to be translated humanly and not merely statistically. A rise of 2 per cent per annum in the average annual income of about $100 per capita represents slightly more than one-half of an American cent per day per person and is the equivalent of, at most, one or two decent extra meals a year. This would affect only microscopically the appalling poverty that prevails among the underdeveloped nations, where poverty is not a pathological deviation from the normal but the ordinary condition in which most of the people must live.

In the underdeveloped region, the second forecast, the inevitability of a rising imperialism (as formulated by Marx, Rosa Luxemburg, and Lenin), also was inaccurate. Facts upset the assumption that highly developed capitalist nations, by reason of internal economic contradictions and the urge for markets and sources of raw materials as well as the lure of bigger profits in "colonial" countries, would be compelled to export capital to the underdeveloped world and so alleviate their own cyclical crises and structural troubles.

The flow of private capital to formerly colonial countries for purely economic reasons has, relatively speaking, ebbed of late, the sole exception being investment in the exploitation of oil wells. However, investment by international and state bodies, such as the World Bank and the American Export-Import Bank, as well as the grants-in-aid of the U.S. government and the financing of development within the ambit of the Colombo Plan and bilateral aid extended by other governments, has gained in importance. All these forms of investment are prompted by political and social motives and have nothing to do with the natural flow of capital from one part of the world to the other, a flow propelled by the force of economic gravitation toward higher returns on capital in countries of cheap labor and proximity to raw materials. The obverse of the coin is that the underdeveloped countries cannot compete in international capital markets for the new capital that is in such tremendous demand in the highly industrialized nations, where the rate of accumulation and savings is incommensurate with the expanding requirement of capital. One cause of this is demographic expansion, which engenders an additional thirst for capital and so, by stimulating demand, galvanizes latent factors of production. The rise in living standards and in consumption in the developed nations emphasizes this trend and contributes to the enlargement of domestic markets.

Under these conditions, the attractiveness of investment in the underdeveloped world, with the political risks that it involves, is rapidly lessening. Moreover, developments in industrialized countries testify abundantly to the truth that prosperity and economic expansion are possible and actually are most pronounced in countries without colonial empires, or that have lost them, such as the United States, West Germany, and the Netherlands. Thus, in the highly industrialized nations that once dominated such empires, resistance to the emancipation of the underdeveloped world is being sapped not only by ideological erosion as democracy and humanism advance and by political considerations inherent in the cold war but also by the economic frustration and futility of colonialism.

Within less than a quarter of a century, India, Indonesia, Indochina, Burma, Ceylon, Israel, Ghana, Nigeria, Tunisia, Morocco, the French colonies, Congo, Cyprus, and other territories won their independence, in some cases after violent struggles, in others by voluntary abdication of the colonial power. The few exceptions were mostly territories where the problem is compounded by a large minority of settlers from the metropolitan country.

Notwithstanding the achievements of military technique—thanks to the shift from man to machine and to highly developed automatic weapons of destruction, which raise the military superiority of the West by providing more efficient tools of suppression—the use of the military apparatus to preserve and perpetuate colonial domination is now progressively of less frequent occurrence, and willing transfer of power to native peoples is today more a rule than an exception.

The third tenet of Marxian doctrine, the increasing frequency of cyclical crises, was also disproved by recent developments. Since 1929, world economy has not experienced a really sharp and abysmal crisis in any way comparable to the Great Depression. After the Second World War, there were a number of recessions, 1949, 1954, and 1958 in the United States, for example, but they were neither deep nor protracted. The built-in stabilizers, of which monetary and fiscal policies are the most significant, are the principal correctives. Monetary policy is a powerful means of regulating the level of economic activity, by rediscount rates, reserve requirements, and open-market operations of the central bank, all of which determine the supply of money. Thus, central banks have the authority and power to influence economic activity by changes in the quantity of money; by their anticyclical policies, they become the bulwark of a directed and guided economy. The tradition of neutrality toward economic processes, of automatic response to purely financial impulses, belongs to the past. Central banks administer an economic policy of clear anticyclical bias that has nothing to do with any reaction to technical challenges of the money market. They are the operators and not the objects of monetary fluctuations. The treasuries of modern states are concerned not only with financing health and education, defense and administration, but to an equal degree with keeping the economy on an even keel and in equilibrium and balance. Countercyclical budgetary policies that steer the economy toward full utilization of all factors of production and full employment or, in changing circumstances of boom and overheated economic activity, combat inflation and welfare policies designed to set bounds to personal misfortune—these have a profound impact on the functioning of the economy.

It is as paradoxical as it is anomalous that the problem of expanding productive forces is already solved in principle, while that of distributing wealth and resources still preoccupies the minds of nations and stamps its plain mark on human conflicts and clashes. Economic science is a more successful agent of rational analysis than it was a decade or two ago. It has forged new, efficient, and workable tools for the shaping of economic conditions and processes that presage with certainty far-reaching social changes. Today, predictions are more solidly based than in the past, and an economy impelled by social aspirations enjoys better guidance.

The plenty of our age and the material saturation in the West face humanity with a new challenge. Mass consumption, hire-purchase, television, cars, suburbia—these adjuncts of modern life are possessed by every industrialized nation.

In the developed world, the advance toward elimination of poverty when measured by relative time-criteria is remarkable: the progress made in the last century toward that end is greater than in the preceding twenty centuries combined. But it is not matched by any comparable improvement in the underdeveloped world. This problem is bound up with the strategy of the war against poverty.

1 *Poverty*

The definition of poverty is one of the most relative and subjective in economic life. Interspatial and intertemporal comparisons point to the tremendous distances between different standards of living. The real problem in analyzing poverty is one of scarcity or insufficiency of resources in some sections of the population and in some areas. In any such analysis, however, only rough approximations are possible, based on averages that conceal more than they reveal, indicating only whether the total of material resources, measured by a subjective standard of what is the subsistence level, is or is not enough. If no insufficiency emerges, then the drop of some sections of the population below subsistence level would reflect only inequality, not scarcity, not a nationwide condition of poverty. So, any model of an economic unit must be broken down into its component parts if meaningful conclusions about absolute and relative poverty are to be arrived at.

In a society whose economic development compelled nature to yield enough of the production necessary for its well-being, poverty signifies a deviation from the average, a kind of social pathology. On the other hand, countries with sparse resources and an average that is unacceptable if measured by empirical and pragmatic social criteria do not reflect a pathological deflection from any average but an absolute dearth of resources. In the last resort, the criteria of analysis here must be historical and pragmatic, based on a socio-economic philosophy and a realistic approach.

capita for the periods 1950–55, 1955–60, and 1960–66 (see Table 1-2).

TABLE 1-2
Per Capita Annual Compound Growth Rates (Per Cent)

	Real gross product per capita		
	1950–55	*1955–60*	*1960–66*
Developed countries	3.6	2.0	3.5
Developing countries	2.8	2.2	2.0

Source: UNCTAD, *Agreed Statement on the Problem of Development,* TD/B/118, Annex 11, para. Ai.

Great technical advances and new economic conditions swelled the GNP of industrialized countries very rapidly, far in excess of the growth of population. The spectacular upswing in standards of living in the highly developed countries was due mainly to a swift and continuous rise in the GNP, with full employment, momentous progress and innovations in technology, and rising productivity as the concomitants. Mounting income and expanding investment stepped up effective demand, which, in turn, acted as a stimulant to economic activity and consequently to economic growth and a bigger GNP.

If we take Engel's Law—the proportion of expenditure on food tends to vary inversely with income—as a point of departure, then, in about 1960, the mean percentage of family expenditure on food ranged from 25 to 30 (Canadian towns, white families in Northern Rhodesia), through 30–35 (northern and western Europe: Sweden, Denmark, Netherlands, Great Britain), 50–55 (the poorer countries of eastern Europe), over 60 (urban populations in parts of North Africa, Asia, and Latin America), to 70–80 in the rural and poorest urban strata of underdeveloped regions.[2] Higher percent-

2 International Labour Office, *Yearbook of Labour Statistics* (Geneva, 1963), tables 22 and 23.

ages occur in abnormally depressed zones, during and after food shortages; lower ones are found among the wealthy.[3]

In the early 1960's, in most Western countries, the considerable margin of underutilization of productive capacity and idle factors of production was contracted or disappeared altogether. The far-flung diffusion of wealth, smaller income differentials, and the social security safeguards, which, during short-lived and mild recessions, were particularly helpful in sustaining effective demand, were instrumental also in keeping up a high level of economic activity and prosperity. Thus, an overall growth of economy and GNP, anticyclical policies shortening and mitigating economic recessions, a social redistribution policy, and social security combined convergingly to quicken demand and raise living standards in developed and industrialized societies.

There could hardly be more conclusive proof of the fallacy of the impoverishment theory. The impulse given to higher living standards by the process described is reinforced, in the same period, by a redistribution of national income. Moreover, the industrial "reserve army" of the proletariat disappears in an ambiance of full employment, minimizing the frictional unemployment that is characteristic of a dynamic economy. This new turn of events means that the proportion of wages and salaries within the national income goes up progressively.

A few representative countries will illustrate this point conclusively. In 1938, in the United States, wages and salaries formed 66.6 per cent of the national income; in 1965, they formed 70 per cent. The corresponding figures for the United Kingdom are even more striking: 62.7 per cent and 74.1 per cent. France had the lowest percentage: 50 in 1938 and 64.9 in 1965. The upward curve of social security and fringe benefits is more pronounced still.

---

[3] U.S. National Resources Committee, *Consumer Expenditures in the United States, Estimates for 1935–36* (1939).

The process of industrialization and urbanization is visible in these statistics, side by side with a constantly larger element of wages within the national income, thanks to the pressure of trade unions, fortified by conditions of full employment, the welfare state, and the mounting political power of labor.

The modern state redistributes national income successfully by its system of progressive taxation, subsidies, old-age, sickness, and unemployment insurance, and an apparatus of social welfare that assures a minimum subsistence in nearly all circumstances and lays a floor below which the income of the poorer classes cannot fall. Consequently, the differences between class standards keep contracting and, even in their extremes, are not nearly as wide as the gap between standards of living in highly industrialized and in underdeveloped countries.

By contrast, the size of the middle classes and their economic weight within the community as a whole have become substantially larger, raising the average income of the population noticeably. The minimum earnings of its less-privileged sections, although still below the average, are on a much higher new level, so that a decidedly smaller percentage lives below what is considered a desirable subsistence level. The very conception of subsistence level has changed a great deal: a much higher standard of living is the target today.

The shift, in developed countries, from the less to the more prosperous classes in demographic make-up and the considerable rise in the subsistence minimum have led to a structural alteration in the pattern of the population. There is an appreciable relative decline of incomes at the top, caused by equalizing systems of taxation and redistribution of the national income; there is a great expansion of the sections enjoying a medium income, and the sections at the lowest income level enjoy a higher minimum standard than in the prewar period.

Moreover, the swelling volume of the GNP in real terms

raises the problem of effective demand, which takes on overwhelming importance for the worker in holding on to his job, to the employer in his search for marketing facilities, and to the state in seeking to prevent acute and prolonged economic recessions and social disturbances.

The dependence of modern economy on effective demand is at odds with policies that try to conceive a labor market based on automatic adjustment of wages to demand and supply and on a proletarian "reserve army" of unemployed. The very term proletariat, in its literal sense, loses all meaning.

It is significant that the report of the special Senate committee on unemployment problems, published on March 30, 1960, affirmed as one of its nine major conclusions that: "High rates of unemployment are not a necessary part of the private enterprise system. Unemployment can be reduced by reasonable private and public policies, as demonstrated by the experience of Great Britain, Sweden, Norway, Finland, the Netherlands, Switzerland, and France."

Higher productivity of labor and the introduction of labor-saving devices mean a migration from the primary to the secondary stage of production and from both to the tertiary, that is, from production of goods to production of services, and incomes rise in close correlation. In the United States, the proliferation of the labor force was accompanied by a fall in the number of workers engaged in the production of goods, and the swing from production of goods to production of services was most marked. In the United States in the period 1929–55, demand for services was nearly equal to demand for goods, but, in the years 1955–59, services multiplied nearly twice as rapidly as production of goods. This development is, among other factors, a reflection of the welfare state, which enlarged the government machinery and caused living standards to rise: this finds expression mainly in services, such as education, health, and travel.

The structural transformation has far-reaching results and is not confined to the sphere of economics but bears also on the pattern of society and of the elements that mold social life. The decline of the blue-collar in comparison with the white-collar working class had not only economic but even more emphatic sociological and psychological repercussions, as discernible in the attitude of labor in highly industrialized countries. Fiscal policies, articulated chiefly in progressive taxation, narrow the economic gap between social classes. Heavy estate duties redistribute wealth. Insurance against unemployment, sickness, and old age minimizes the influence of depressants on the living standards of individuals and of entire social classes alike. Diffusion of ownership through the corporation and the stock exchange and the rise of the middle class are additional stimuli of this economic reshuffle of modern society. Social polarization and impoverishment are stillborn thanks to the welfare state and the policy of egalitarianism, technical progress, and the emergence of the middle classes.

Economic power is becoming divorced from proprietary rights by the development of public and private corporations. In a joint stock company, the manager and not the shareholder wields sovereignty. Rising technocracy and the managerial elite are the backbone of modern forms of economy and state.

Because of the power of trade unions, the welfare state, and the new trend in more prosperous, more socially conscious, and more liberal societies, improved standards of living and the per capita growth of the GNP are a self-perpetuating process. Moreover, in a mixed economy with a large government or semi-government sector, normative and purposive economics aiming to abolish poverty in developed countries can dispose of a more numerous array of levers of economic power directed toward that end.

The greater weight and importance of the government sector in a modern economy in comparison with the last century, or even the 1920's and 1930's, influence economic activity and are compensatory factors and stimulants whenever that activity slackens or investment in the private sector falters. The radius of the swing of the economic pendulum is thus being shortened. The employment generated by the rise in government purchases and in home building and the large benefit payments by the state help many of the unemployed to keep their heads financially above water. That is why total personal income dropped little during the postwar recessions in the United States. Consumers and government did much to sustain a fairly high level of demand during those recessions and were instrumental in the recoveries that followed them. Personal income was held at a substantial figure, and consumers could thus keep to and even step up their spending on nondurable goods. Nearly half of the drop in private income in the United States between August, 1957, and April, 1958, for example, was offset by increased government disbursements such as unemployment allowances, and large outlay of public works by state and local authorities lessened the effects of the business slump and contributed to economic convalescence.

A method defined in economic terminology as pump priming, which would have been anathema to an orthodox economist in the nineteenth century, is now the legitimate tool of economic policy, with many and varied techniques simplifying its use. On top of it, the progressive system of taxation prevents any contraction of purchasing power and effective demand *pari passu* with contraction of economic activity. So, in times of recession, the cutting down of incomes is much less drastic than the circumscription of business. Demand is kept going by official and consumer expenditure. Welfare disbursements and unemployment insurance also neutralize any tendency toward a too rapid and too sharp diminution of purchasing power. All these instruments, controlled by governments and central banks, provide a degree of flexibility that is essential in times of recession.

The fear that social security could affect productivity and slow up its progress was dispelled by the realities of the situation. There is ample statistical and empirical evidence that not only did that not happen, but that, in the last two decades, the spread of social security was integral to the progress of productivity. Application of macroeconomic measures to soften economic setbacks and built-in stabilizers achieved the dual effect of narrowing the amplitude and abridging the duration of recessions.

The Marxian conception, based as it was on forebodings of impoverishment, of expansion of imperialism, and of higher frequency of cyclical crises, was grandiose in its great sweep, but it could not stand the test of economic facts, and, together with certain tenets of the classical economic tradition, was disproved by the realities of the twentieth century. It wrongly assumed a completely free market economy with no interference by political or conscious economic forces. It presupposed the working of a perfect, competitive, capitalist society, which did not exist in reality in pure and undiluted form. In fact, modern economy was transformed gradually by the impact of new economic conditions. Conscious intervention in the mechanism of economy and society went so far that market mechanics had to undergo a fundamental change. The naked mechanism of a free market economy envisaged by the "dismal science" has never seen the light. The reforming zeal of the rebels of the nineteenth century was carried over into our period, but with a new, nonrevolutionary twist that led to a managed and guided economy that does not heed the precepts of unadulterated free market capitalism.

Between the two world wars, the economy of most developed countries was buffeted by alternating bouts of inflation, in many cases runaway inflation, which ruined the middle classes, particularly those relying on fixed incomes, and of deflation, which led to widespread unemployment and depressed the living standards of labor. In 1933, the GNP of the United States, at current prices, was only 71 per cent of its 1929 volume, and the number of unemployed had neared 13 million. The lengthening radius of the swinging pendulum of boom and slump had ubiquitous social and political repercussions.

The idea of guiding and directing the economy was tabu to most economists until then. The surplus capacity of production was idle and underutilized. Monetary policy clung stubbornly to the gold standard, and automatic readjustments did not meet the exigencies of an entirely new situation. Effective demand lagged far behind actual production. Decline of prices, accumulation of inert deposits and savings, contraction of the market and of investment, underemployment of labor and of other factors of production were of only too frequent occurrence.

Later, however, the theory was evolved that hibernating factors of production could be galvanized by monetary and fiscal policies, expanding productive scope and dimension by a reallocation of resources as between investment and consumption and trespassing on the sacrosanct automatism and autonomy of the economic mechanism. This school of thought rejected the gold standard as a basis of monetary policy and defined it as an obsolete "barbaric relic," which had outlived its usefulness in a modern economy and allowed for deficit financing of government budgets in times of deep depression and for surpluses in times of boom, simultaneously resisting an all-out nationalization of means of production and the conception of an economy planned not only in quantitative, but also in qualitative, terms.

The authors of the new thinking, and particularly the most prominent of them, John Maynard Keynes, believed that the economic problem of material scarcity could be solved, given three conditions: power to control the growth of population, elimination of the danger of a major war, and a properly balanced distribution of resources between investment and consumption.

The discussion between Montagu Norman and Keynes threw into bold relief the contrast between two economic, social, and political philosophies. At that juncture, the desire to reach economic equilibrium meant first and foremost the ending of deflationary stagnation. The developments in the United States after the crisis, the changes in several European countries that adopted the system of quantitative economic controls, the method of cyclical budgets balancing over a number of years and not annually, and so on, all belied the pessimistic forecast of the early 1930's.

Conclusions of economic policy resulting from the new outlook in the 1930's were geared to a particular condition of the world economy, affected at that period of time by a deflationary crisis. Still, seeds of a more universal theory germinated in the new conception, the theory of a managed balance, which would also apply to periods of inflation and of overheated economic activity, although with a variant twist in methods of implementation. The greatest mistake of some of Keynes' interpreters was to oversimplify his theory, confining it to certain circumstances and limiting its application to a deflationary crisis. In fact, its meaning is much more applicable. The theory and method of thinking and analysis evolved out of a deflationary crisis can serve equally well as a point of departure for policy in a totally different situation, namely, in periods of excessive pressure of effective demand on limited resources producing an inflationary crisis. This adaptability of the new theory to diametrically divergent situations is its special value.

The realities from which the new theory sprang largely disappeared with the outbreak of the Second World War. During the fighting, an immense expansion of production took place, but the new resources had to be dedicated to the

war effort, and so, in spite of that expansion, the war economy
was one of scarcity and shortages. A sharp turn of the rudder
was required. Consumption had to be curtailed and resources
diverted to campaign needs. The value of the Keynesian theory and its application to a situation unlike that prevailing
in the 1920's and 1930's were manifested amply. The weapons
to combat deflation and the analysis of the economy previously made had now to answer the opposite purpose—pre-
venting inflation. Keynes explained the fresh implications of
his theory, illustrating how to reestablish the balance in the
reverse direction when effective demand exerts an irresistible
pressure on scarce resources.

The concept of a guided economy is universal. It reflects
observation of certain disparities and disequilibria that stem
from the automatic, self-propelled working of the economy's
mechanism. It tries to activate countervailing forces, on the
assumption that laggard factors of production can be quickened by monetary and fiscal policies. When the theory was
first formulated, it represented an attempt to overcome dis-
crepancies due to effective demand trailing behind expansion
of productive capacity, faltering investment, depression, deflation, and stagnation. But this application of it was a result
of certain temporary conditions and was not inherent in its
premises. On the same premises, a different policy could be
and was worked out in a period when imbalances and disparities in the economy were generated by processes of inflation,
overexpansion, too rapid growth of effective demand, and the
like. That different and contrary policies could be fash-
ioned and applied on this basis under vastly dissimilar conditions was proof of the usefulness of the theory in changing
circumstances.

The judgment that this analysis has outlived its usefulness
under new conditions of postwar economy turns on an inter-
pretation that confuses the universal theory with its particular
application in the interwar period, whereas its very analysis

and conclusions are conducive to a judgment under different conditions. Just as the aftermath of the Second World War differed from that of the First World War, so did the policies evolved on the strength of the same theory in each of those periods differ. Toward the end of the interwar period, in a time of instability caused by deflation, shakiness of investment, and ebbing of effective demand, with unemployment and stagnation on their heels, the theory of economic guidance laid stress on the stimulation of expansionist forces, reflation, cheap money, credit expansion, and government incentives to economic activity, if necessary by deficit financing of the state budget.

After the Second World War, under conditions of great liquidity in the economy and a pent-up effective demand, of disparities and imbalances caused by inflationary pressures, boom conditions, and overfull employment, the emphasis is on containment of inflationary pressures, curbs on the rise of individual incomes—that is, wages and salaries in the main—a balanced budget, a disinflationary monetary policy, credit restriction, and dearer money. Whenever economic activity limps, governments and central banks embark on an active policy, among other things ensuring a fuller utilization of resources and full employment, contracting by fiscal devices the space between different scales of income, establishing by welfare state measures a minimum for incomes, making cyclical recessions briefer and milder and shortening the radius of the swinging pendulum of boom and slump, assuring a maximum and sustained growth of the GNP, and encouraging a flow of capital to underdeveloped countries to hasten the growth of their economies.

The flight from crude methods of direct physical and administrative controls led to the improvement and perfection of more subtle and effective ones, chiefly through the fiscal and monetary policies affecting the total aggregate demand. Instead of goods being rationed, the supply of money is made flexible, restricted or expanded to conform with the growth of the GNP. Monetary and fiscal policies, although unpopular, are refined and are not only more effective and all-pervading but also less annoying and cumbersome than physical and administrative controls. They have the advantage, too, that they do not entail distortions in the structure of prices, production, or investment. They limit the freedom of the individual much less stringently. In a modern economy, the free market and the consumers' choice determine the composition of goods and services consumed, but the extent of production, consumption, and investment and the allocation of resources are influenced decisively by instruments of monetary and fiscal policy. Government, local authorities, public and semi-public bodies are assuming ever wider and more numerous responsibilities in the economic and social life of every developed country. It is estimated that, in most countries of the West, the public sector, in which the principal economic decisions are taken by the state through its budget or by other means, today forms about one-third of the total economy and is constantly encroaching.

The method and machinery of economic control are subject to radical change. The economy is expanding rapidly. New capital is raised more and more by institutional savings. Insurance companies, investment funds, trust and pension funds, unemployment funds, compensation funds, and so forth are a large source of capital for financing industry and the economy at large. Present levels of taxation, which take care of social security and the welfare state, would have been deemed unattainable only a generation ago. The legend that the financing of the welfare state has placed a monstrous burden on the middle classes is controverted by the remarkable rise in the living standards of that population group, which, furthermore, is now of quite large numbers.

The figures in the Radcliffe Report show that the gross debt of the public sector in Britain (central government, nationalized institutions, and local authorities) rose from £9,111 million in 1935 to £41,105 million in 1958. Capital expenditure of the central government was £41 million in 1938 and £243 million in 1958.

In the United States, the federal government is more and more responsible for setting the pace at which the national economy ought to expand. The state is committed to strengthening the social security system, "the floor over the pit of personal disaster."

The share of taxation in the national income of the United States was 19.6 per cent in 1938 and 33.8 per cent in 1965; in Britain it was 25.0 per cent and 37.9 per cent respectively.

The First National City Bank of New York, in its monthly letter of June, 1960, quotes the following figures, which reveal the growing part of the state in the American economy:[4] federal cash expenditure, which was $2.8 billion in the mid-1920's and $9.6 billion in 1940, was $94.8 billion in the late 1950's; state and local government expenditure amounted to $7.7 billion and $10.3 billion respectively in the mid-1930's and in 1940, and rose to $48.8 billion in the late 1950's; the corresponding figures for the GNP are $97.6 billion, $95.6 billion, and $463.8 billion. Social insurance benefits, $1,215 million in 1940, were $15,975 million by the late 1950's; highway expenditures rose from $1,819 million in 1920 to $8,702 million some twelve years later, and aid to other transportation rose from $257 million to $1,629 million; in the same period, expenditure on public welfare and assistance expanded from $161 million to $3,777 million; federal expenditure on health, which was $84 million in the mid-1920's and $105 million in 1940, was $806 million in the late 1950's; the corresponding figures for hospitals are $347 million, $537 million, and $3,849 million; and, for educa-

---

4 The figures are taken from the U.S. Census Bureau's *Surveys of Governmental Finances in the United States;* the U.S. Department of Health, Education, and Welfare's *Health, Education and Welfare Trends;* and other official publications.

tion, $2,243 million, $2,827 million, and $16,836 million. There were 4.2 million personal income tax returns in the mid-1920's and 14.8 million in 1940; by the late 1950's, the number had risen to 59.8 million. Government employment went up from 2.8 million in the mid-1920's to 4.2 million in 1940 and 8.1 million some twenty years later. In 1940, 60.9 thousand public housing units were constructed; by the late 1950's, 444.7 thousand had been built. This is evidence of state control of more and more of the national income and concurrent state concern for the satisfaction of a growing range and scope of the population's needs, pointing to magnification of state authority in the economic life of a modern country and state penetration of all spheres of that life.

In the West, the idea of economic and social engineering, which can progressively condition the life of society, is gaining ground in a constantly larger variety of areas of enterprise and life. Moreover, ideological resistance to the welfare state and to state intervention in economic life is weakening. In this context, it is pertinent to quote from a speech by Ambassador Henry Cabot Lodge, Jr., in greeting the Soviet Premier Nikita Khrushchev in September, 1959:

> American business prospers at the same time that the federal government, in ways large and small, pervades our lives—that one adult in every five gets regular checks from the government and that countless others receive occasional payments, that federal warehouses give out food to more than five million persons —and that two million persons live in government-subsidized housing. . . . We live in a welfare state which seeks to put a floor below which no one sinks, but builds no ceiling to prevent man from rising.

The technological revolution in the twentieth century changed human life more than any event since the emergence of man on the earth's surface. The combustion engine and the jet plane, agents of man's almost unlimited mobility on that surface; the new media of mass communication—cinema, radio, and television; atomic energy and the atomic and hydrogen bombs—nuclear weapons of mass destruction; satellites and penetration of outer-stellar space; the discovery of antibiotics and the unfolding mystery of modern biology and chemistry; the uplift in global productive capacity; automation; electronics: these wonders have had an impact on the individual and on society beyond all imagining. It is a far cry from the steam engine and the leisurely tempo of progress of the Victorian age to this turbulent, discordant, confused, and frightening planet of ours. But no nostalgic yearning after the easeful and idyllic past can turn the clock back. On its journey into the unknown, man cannot return.

In this setting, the forces working toward the abolition of poverty in developed countries are part of the economic and social mechanisms. The most recent expression of the tendency is the notion of a national system of income guarantees and supplements, the so-called negative income tax, which would ultimately extinguish poverty, as empirical and pragmatic criteria conceive and define it.

The following proclamation, signed in 1968 by a thousand economists, among them Galbraith and Samuelson, and delivered to the Joint Economic Committee of the Congress, sets out the main ideas of "income guarantees and supplements":

The undersigned economists urge the Congress to adopt this year a national system of income guarantees and supplements.

The Poor People's Campaign in Washington is demanding a guaranteed minimum income for all Americans. The Kerner Commission on Civil Disorders called for a national system of income supplements. A group of business leaders recently advocated a "negative income tax." These proposals are all similar in design and purpose.

Like all civilized nations in the 20th century, this country has long recognized a public responsibility for the living standards of its citizens. Yet our present programs of public assistance and social insurance exclude millions who are in need and meet in-

adequately the needs of millions more. All too often these programs unnecessarily penalize work and thrift and discourage
the building of stable families.

The country will not have met its responsibility until every-
one in the nation is assured an income no less than the officially
recognized definition of poverty. A workable and equitable plan
of income guarantees and supplements must have the following
features. (1) Need, as objectively measured by income and family size, should be the sole basis of determining payment to
which an individual and/or family is entitled. (2) To provide incentive to work, save, and train for better jobs, payments to
families who earn income should be reduced by only a fraction
of their earnings.

Practical and detailed proposals meeting these requirements
have been suggested by individual sponsors of this statement and
by others. The costs of such plans are substantial but well within
the nation's economic and fiscal capacity.

As economists we offer the professional opinion that income
guarantees and supplements are feasible and compatible with
our economic system. As citizens we feel strongly that the time
for action is now.

The system of income guarantees and supplements would
encounter its main difficulty not because of the scarcity of
economic resources but in the realm of sociology and psychology. The disparity between the psychology and theory of the
economics of want and the reality of an affluent society is the
chief hurdle on the path to abolition of poverty. The guaranteed minimum income would have to be flexible enough to
prevent people's sinking below the poverty line and yet not
so flexible as to arrest the driving force of economic incentive.

This problem is not insoluble. Experience shows that, as
a rule, even with an assured minimum of subsistence, the impulsion of the wish to raise the standard of living and to
climb in the social hierarchy is powerful enough to stimulate
economic enterprise and endeavor. The line will have to be
drawn carefully to keep that impulsion going, and here the
problem is mostly quantitative, although, in all circumstances,

marginal cases of weakened incentives, which the economy can well afford, will be unavoidable.

Thus, the problem in the developed world is how to deal with the revolution of rising expectations in countries that, though rich by world standards, are not rich enough to meet the rocketing demands of their citizens. The dangers are not of social polarization and economic impoverishment, but of inflation and excessive expansion of domestic consumption. They are the dangers of an inward-looking economy that disregards overall global desiderata.

Barring unforeseen circumstances, the GNP of the developed world should reach nearly $2,300 billion in the early 1970's. Dispersal of the increment should be subject to weighty social and political pressures, apexing in the establishment of a floor of guaranteed income-minimum, the so-called income maintenance system. Implementation of that system, which would assure a standard of living for everyone equivalent to opulence in terms of the underdeveloped nations, could be achieved today at a far from crippling, even though very sizeable, cost. Thus, in the long run, in the developed and technological society, victory in the war against poverty is a foregone conclusion. A few redistributive measures, such as the income maintenance system, parallel with the constant per capita rise in the GNP, would herald the age of plenty. Thus viewed, the problem of the underdeveloped two-thirds of humanity assumes a crucial significance.

For realization of the scope and depth of this problem, it suffices to present a few indications, such as those of annual income per head, nutritional standards, and expectancy of life. The President of the World Bank, Robert S. McNamara, said: "The average annual per capita income in some forty of the world's poorest countries today is roughly $120. That is less than 35 cents a day. The annual per capita income in the United States is nearly $3,000. That is about $8.00 a day.

That is more than a 2000 per cent difference."[5] These are averages, in underdeveloped countries, between the ricksha-pulling coolie toiling in the tracks of a beast of burden and a maharajah or a Western millionaire.

Specific data are not less illuminating:

> In 1964 the gross domestic product per head of the population, and expressed in dollars, amounted to 73 in Congo (Kinshasa), 74 in South Vietnam, 124 in Belgium, 144 in Bolivia, 428 in Mexico, 718 in Japan, 1,462 in Belgium, 2,071 in Switzerland, 2,095 in Sweden, 3,002 in the U.S.A. More recent data allow us to infer that these very considerable differences increase rather than decrease.[6]

The economic disparity between the developed and the underdeveloped world is glaringly reflected even in the con-

TABLE 1-3
Consumption of Primary Calories per Day, 1960

Less-developed regions	
Population (millions)	2,022
Consumption per person	
Calories	2,150
Animal protein (grams)	9
Animal food (calories)	180
Plant food (calories)	1,970
Primary calories	3,230
More-developed regions	
Population (millions)	974
Consumption per person	
Calories	3,050
Animal protein (grams)	44
Animal food (calories)	880
Plant food (calories)	2,170
Primary calories	8,330

Source: OECD, *The Food Problem of Developing Countries* (Paris, 1968), p. 34.

[5] Robert S. McNamara, "Toward the Prevention of Seismic Social Shock," address delivered on February 24, 1967.

[6] Flemish Economic Association, *Development Aid,* Eighth Scientific Congress of Flemish Economists (Ghent: May 19–20, 1967).

sumption of basic necessities, as the data in Table 1-3 evince.

The disparities in life expectancy are as striking. In the underdeveloped regions, the expectation at birth is around 40–45 in Africa, 45–50 in Asia, and 55–60 in Latin America. In developed countries, it is around 64–75 years.

Unemployment and underemployment are among the worst plagues of the underdeveloped world, and the trend is one of steady worsening.

> One of the most serious problems facing the developing countries is increasing underemployment and unemployment. This increase is not confined to countries already experiencing population pressures, although rapidly rising population is undoubtedly a major aggravating factor. Far-reaching action will be required if the fruits of economic progress are to benefit all the inhabitants of the world.[7]

These are the hard facts and harsh realities of life in present circumstances. The basic fact stands: in the underdeveloped nations, poverty is not a pathological deviation from the normal and normative but the state of affairs and the set of conditions under which the overwhelming majority of people are compelled to live. The most striking instance of these conditions is represented by India:

> In these circumstances, India has no choice and no escape; we must control our population growth. While we must make every effort to step up the rate of our economic development and growth—and we are making such efforts—there is no doubt that to get the necessary increases in per capita income and improvememnts in the standard of living, the present rate of increase in population must be checked, and checked drastically. The Indian per capita income, as is well known, is one of the lowest in the world—even after 14 years of planned development and prodigious efforts by our people and assistance from abroad, our per capita annual income today is only $80,

7 U.N. Department of Economic and Social Affairs, *The United Nations Development Decade, Proposals for Action,* Report of the Secretary-General, Doc. E/3613 (New York, 1962), p. vii.

which works out to a little more than 20 cents a day. In the developed countries people eating three good meals a day spend more than that on a snack to keep them going between lunch and dinner. Again, as the 20 cents a day is an average, millions of people in India get much less. Though foodstuffs and clothing and such essentials are fortunately much cheaper in India than in the industrialized countries, it is still hard for people elsewhere even to imagine what deprivations, hunger, and lack of the barest necessities of life these scores of millions of people have to suffer all their lives.[8]

The aftermath of this adverse development will be the aggravation of a second problem, food supply. The U.N. Food and Agriculture Organization defines the situation as follows:

Any remaining complacency about the food and agriculture situation must surely have been dispelled by the events of the past year. As a result of widespread drought, world food production, according to FAO's preliminary estimates, was no larger in 1965/66 than the year before, when there were about 70 million less people to feed. . . . Thus the world food situation is now more precarious than at any time since the period of acute shortage immediately after the Second World War.[9]

The effects of malnutrition on the physique and health of children are particularly distressing:

Central Africa provides an illuminating example: about 50 per cent of the children from weaning age to school age die. One-third of these deaths is attributable to protein deficiency, although hunger is satisfied because of ample bulk of starchy foods. The protein-poor diet denies them amino acids essential for normal growth and development. Results are either death from kwashiorkor or marasmus, or stunted growth, mental retardation, and susceptibility to infectious diseases.

[8] K. S. Sundara Rajan, "India's Population Problem," *Finance and Development*, Vol. 2 (September, 1965), p. 145.
[9] U.N. Food and Agriculture Organization, *The State of Food and Agriculture, 1966*, Doc. CL 47/2 (Rome, 1966), p. 1.

The disparity in protein consumption, widespread in Egypt, India, South America, and other developing countries, thus becomes catastrophic. In terms of pure, dry protein, the annual deficit of animal protein is estimated at about 10 million metric tons by 1970.[10]

Famine is an economic problem. Physically, the world is able to provide food and proper nutrition for all mankind and even to yield surplus agricultural produce. But "hunger is a problem which extends far beyond the field of food and agriculture alone. It can be readily and effectively eliminated only by abolishing poverty."[11]

Another focus of present dynamics is on investment, of which economic growth and production per head are to a great extent the function. The yearly gross capital investment per head is $354 in the developed and $42 in the developing countries, meaning a ratio of 1 : 8.5, which—should it be perpetuated—augurs a melancholy future.[12] Accordingly, the scope and direction of investments signify a swift and sharp widening of the gap between the populations of the two parts of the world, whose quantitative ratio at the end of this century will be 1 : 4.

Let us summarize the developmental trends in each of the focal points of the dynamics of development. First, the population growth in the developing countries is put at some 2.5 per cent per annum. The world's total population will double by the end of the century, but about two-thirds of it lives in the developing regions and half of it on the Asian continent. The speedy rise of population in the underdeveloped areas exerts an intolerable pressure on limited resources, and in those areas the pressure is most pronounced. World leaders declared in December, 1967:

10 George B. Sumyk, "The Third Horseman," *Frontier*, Vol. 27 (Summer, 1966), p. 6.

11 *The United Nations Development Decade*, p. 44.

12 United Nations, *Yearbook of National Accounts Statistics, 1966* (New York, 1967).

The population problem must be recognized as a principal element in long-range national planning and the too rapid population growth seriously hampers efforts to raise living standards, to further education, to improve health and sanitation, to
provide better housing and transportation, to forward cultural
and recreational opportunities—and even in some countries to
assure sufficient food.

Consequently, at the end of this century, it will be more difficult to bridge the gap between the two parts of the world,
and the burden of bridging it will have to be shouldered by
a smaller section of the highly developed population.

Second, the income gap will be greater because of the increased proportion of the world's population living in underdeveloped countries and the inadequacy of the rise of the
GNP per capita in those countries to catch up with the pace
of its rise in the developed ones.

Economic growth is chiefly a function of investment. As
long as investment per head in developed countries is 8.5
times higher than in underdeveloped ones, the gap between
the two parts of the world will quickly increase. The problem is aggravated in some cases by technological progress,
which swells the volume of capital that has to be invested per
head to achieve significant economic growth. Moreover, the
composition of investment in this age of advanced technology
necessitates a multiplication of the components of skill, know-
how, and higher education, which are in short supply in
underdeveloped countries. Economic growth in our time demands a larger unit of equipment per head and a larger proportion of skilled manpower, know-how, and specialization of
workers than it did in the past. Thus, the problem of abolition of poverty must be seen today against the background of
the emergence of the system of new economics and the swifter
pace of progress of modern technology.

There is no doubt that, in developed countries, the rapid
economic growth, the limited rise of population, and the re-

distribution of incomes through the welfare state have led to a real reduction of income differentials, established standards of high and rising incomes, and prevented social polarization. Democratic, political, and economic pressures safeguard these trends, which make poverty a marginal phenomenon by any pragmatic and empirical yardstick. Poverty in the developed countries is a symptom of social pathology and a deviation from the average. It is the result of the imperfection of social and economic mechanisms and is by no means inevitable. Economic growth is adequate in terms of national and per capita totals, and should assure a self-perpetuating tendency toward elimination of poverty. Anyhow, whatever the criterion, the poverty line would be regarded as affluence in any underdeveloped country.

The new economy and modern technology and the social redistribution devices confirm the truth that, if socio-economic readjustment is carried to its logical conclusion by a system of income maintenance and guarantees of minimum incomes, society, by these redistributive measures, could be freed of marginal deviations from satisfactory averages. The dynamics of that process are self-perpetuating, and, fortified by measures of economic policy, the process should, in the course of time, bring about the abolition of poverty in the developed world.

This is not so in the underdeveloped world, where scarcity is absolute, not relative. No redistributive mechanism would assure a minimum of subsistence to its populations. Poverty there is not a pathological, marginal phenomenon, but a structural problem. The total growth is insufficient and per capita slightly more than half of what it is in developed countries, starting from an already too low level. The annual increment is negligible, and the dynamics tend to enlarge the gap of inequality with the developed world and make the low levels of income and consumption permanent. Impoverishment becomes a self-propelling, dynamic process.

In this light, the question is whether the new economics and modern technology are capable of coping with a problem that intrinsically is structural and economic and not likely to lend itself to treatment by methods of social welfare.

By force of these circumstances, what is needed is a strategy of economic development, and, in the first instance, that problem hinges on three economic factors: manpower, capital, and effective demand.

2 Population

In the underdeveloped areas of the world, the population explosion seems to be one of the most important single causes of retarded economic progress. Concentration of an unprecedented growth of population in continents and in countries where it exerts the strongest pressure on resources, the realities and projection of famine, the correlation of overpopulation and misery, the virtual stagnation in economic growth per head of population: these are warning signals on a global scale. The situation is well described below:

The belief is spreading that economic development in the poor countries of the world will never make much headway until their population growth is slowed down. Many economists and demographers have long believed this, but the acceleration of demographic growth in the developing countries has accentuated the issue and made it seem that the remarkable economic expansion which has been achieved in many of these countries merely serves to keep larger populations at the same low levels of welfare. The extraordinary projections of the future growth of population in the world, and especially in the underdeveloped part of the world, have also enormously enhanced the awareness of the population explosion. But above all, those who in the developing countries have been given the responsibility of planning their economic and social advance have, by their experiences and their calculations, been forced to a realization of the burdens that population growth of 2–3 per cent a year imposes on their countries. At such rates a population doubles in 25 years; this doubles the requirements of facilities they would like to provide in the form of schools, hospitals, and housing; conversely it cuts in half the benefits of what they might expect to provide in that time. . . .

With the present trend of accelerating growth it would only take another hundred years for mankind to cover the inhabitable parts of the world with an average density greater than that of today's Holland. Science and technology may in the end make it possible to sustain an even more densely settled world than that, but even the most generous estimates of the ultimate carrying capacity of the world would be attained in less time than separates us from the European discovery of the rest of the world.[1]

The economic growth rates per capita in the developed and underdeveloped worlds and the gulf between them are highly significant. The data in Table 2-1 reflect this.

TABLE 2-1

Per Cent Annual Growth Rates of Real Gross Product in Developing and Developed Countries, 1950–66

	GNP	GNP per capita
Developing countries*	4.6	2.3
Asia	4.1	1.9
Latin America	4.9	2.1
Developed countries (market economies)	4.3	3.1
Socialist countries of eastern Europe†	8.2	6.8

* Includes African and Middle Eastern countries.
† Gross material product.

Source: UNCTAD, *Growth and External Development Finance,* TD 7, Supp. 1 (October, 1967).

Two basic facts emerge: first, the average rates of growth in the developed and underdeveloped countries differ overall only very slightly; second, the adverse developments in the economic conditions of the underdeveloped countries and the slow material progress of that world are mainly caused by the population explosion. The causes of this explosion are, para-

[1] Goran Ohlin, *Population Control and Economic Development* (Paris: Development Center of the Organization of Economic Cooperation and Development, 1967), pp. 7, 11.

doxically, the progress of hygiene and medical care, which brought about a rapid and steep decline in mortality rates, particularly in infant mortality, while birth rates have not declined at all.

Table 2-2 presents the rates of population growth in the world as a whole and in the more-developed and developing regions. More-developed regions include North America, temperate South America, Europe, Japan, Australia, and New Zealand. Developing regions include Africa, East Asia (excluding Japan), South Asia, Latin America (excluding temperate South America), Melanesia, Polynesia, and Micronesia. Note the tendency for population growth to gather momentum in the 1950's.

TABLE 2-2
Per Cent Annual Rate of Growth

Period	World	More-developed regions	Developing regions
1920–30	1.0	1.2	1.0
1930–40	1.0	0.8	1.2
1940–50	0.9	0.4	1.2
1950–60	1.8	1.3	2.0

Source: United Nations, Population Division, New York; and Goran Ohlin, *Population Control and Economic Development* (Paris: Development Center of the Organization of Economic Cooperation and Development, 1967), p. 12.

It would seem that the regional distribution of demographic growth deviates from the economic optimum, being concentrated in countries with scarce resources and an already excessive pressure of population. While rates of economic growth are similar in the developed and underdeveloped worlds, the population growth neutralizes the effect of a rising GNP on the economic conditions and welfare of developing populations. India is a vivid example of this development.

How much of our development effort is absorbed by the increase in population will be seen from the fact that though our national income has increased during the last 15 years from $18.42 billion to $31.19 billion (at constant prices), or by 68 per cent, our per capita income has goné up by only 25 per cent. . . . Indeed, because of the rapidly increasing population, we in India, like the other developing countries, are running up an escalator that is marked "Down."[2]

It has been calculated that, to close the gap between the developed and underdeveloped worlds in seventy-five years, the rate of growth of the GNP per capita in most underdeveloped countries would have to range between 5 and 6.5 per cent per annum, which is about 2.5 to 3 times the present rate.[3]

The consequences of the demographic process are evident. First, hunger and malnutrition, of which—as President Johnson said—the result is this: "The world food problem is one of the foremost challenges of mankind today. The dimension of the challenge will define the dimension of our response and the means for that response. We must join with others in a massive effort to help the less fortunate of the earth to help themselves."[4] Second, widespread unemployment and underemployment, particularly in the rural economy. Third, slow capital formation, which does not yield means enough to overcome the obstacle created by the tardiness of economic growth. Fourth, an educational lag, with ignorance alongside it, a special handicap in a modern technological economy. Fifth, widespread disease and physical disability, which affect efficiency and skill in the performance of economic tasks, perpetuating current conditions of back-

[2] K. S. Sundara Rajan, "India's Population Problem," *Finance and Development,* Vol. 2 (September, 1965), p. 146.
[3] Ernest Lamers, "How Fast Will the Gap Close?" *International Development Review,* Vol. 9 (March, 1967), p. 3.
[4] Report of the World Food Panel of the U.S. President's Science Advisory Committee, Vol. 1 (Washington, D.C., June, 1967).

wardness and economic deterioration in various sectors of the population.

The sinister link between the high rates of natural increase of the populations of the developing regions and their appalling poverty is unmistakable; the causative nexus between low rates of economic growth per capita and their demographic expansion is borne out by facts and figures. Under such conditions, the likelihood of an economic breakthrough and of rising standards of living is discouragingly dim. In an address delivered at the 1968 annual meeting of the World Bank, IFC, and IDA, Robert S. McNamara, president of the World Bank, said:

> . . . economic studies show that this drag of excessive population growth is quite independent of the density of population. This is something that needs emphasizing in view of the fact that many policy-makers in the developing countries attach only minor importance to reducing population growth. It is a false claim that some countries need more population to fill their land or accelerate their economic growth. There are no vacant lands equipped with roads, schools, houses, and the tools of agricultural or industrial employment. Therefore, the people who are to fill those lands, before they can live at even the current low standards of living, must first eat up a portion of the present scarce supply of capital—it is this burden which defeats a nation's efforts to raise its standard of living by increasing its population.

In a speech before the Economic and Social Council of the United Nations in December, 1968, McNamara said:

> In one poor country after another, the rising tide of population swamps the school system, literally eats away the margin of saving, and inundates the labor market. No power on earth can ensure that there will be such rapid economic progress that all today's children will grow up healthy, well educated, and able to take their rightful place in a competitive world. If development efforts are to succeed—not development of such

abstractions as "the economy" or "the state," but development of human beings, of individuals and families—we must put population policy at the center of our future strategy.

The demographic problem is one not so much of space or even of natural resources but of capital and skill, of mobile resources. A rapid rise in population, if linked with an adequate supply of capital and skill, can work as a stimulant of economic growth.

The data on rates of growth of population and GNP are an index of the dynamic sequence of events but do not answer the question whether anything like the concept of absolute overpopulation could be applied to the areas concerned. Empirical analysis of the data offers no evidence that such a neo-Malthusian concept is borne out by facts, whatever criteria be applied to measure the disparity between numbers and natural resources. The emphasis here is on the definition of "natural" resources, resources with no mobility at all.

To select criteria of overpopulation is no easy matter; the optimum relation of population to resources is vague and undefinable. It is doubtful if it can ever be gauged in arithmetic terms. It is the function of a large number of variables, which in turn depend on the particular experience of each individual country. Any calculation must be limited to the immediate future, whether the point of departure is consumption and marketing possibilities or the expansion of production. Each phase of development is a vector of new problems and new possibilities unpredictable in advance. Sismondi says: "The true problem of the statesman is to find the combination and the ratio of population to wealth which will assure most happiness to the human race on a given area."[5]

[5] Jean C. L. Simonde de Sismondi, *Nouveaux Principes d'Economie Politique,* second edition, Vol. 2, ch. 5.

However, the complex character of modern economy makes that task exceedingly difficult. Transformation of economic conditions, technical discoveries and inventions, development of potential resources, and shifts in consumption and in marketing facilities must be considered. Such variables as capital and scientific and technical knowledge are subject to almost never-ending change and metamorphosis. The factors of cultural and technical level, economic and social systems, structure and quality of population, and occupational distribution and the dynamic interaction of them all are of countless variety.

Fergus Chalmers Wright stresses the fact that

> . . . whatever the method employed, it must be recognized . . . that surface area is only one, and a decreasingly important aspect, of the natural physical environment which conditions population density; climate, topography, location, the physical constituents of the soil, sub-surfaces, supplies of minerals and fuels and a number of other natural physical factors are equally as important as land area. Moreover, such an index entirely neglects the artificial, physical environment, as well as technological, economic and social conditions of paramount importance in conditioning population growth. To impute under- or overpopulation by relating the residents of a region to one of many portions of one of many aspects of the total environment would seem on a priori grounds to be not only unscientific but misleading.[6]

Interaction of population with the physical background of the country and their repercussions one upon the other cannot be disregarded. To the same extent to which a country's economic capacity in relation to its population is determined by its attributes, so are those attributes transformed by the growth of that population, its character, propensities, and

[6] Fergus Chalmers Wright, "The Ability of Canada to Receive Immigration," *Peaceful Change, Population and Peace* (Paris: International Institute of Intellectual Cooperation, League of Nations, 1939), p. 72.

standards, its efficiency and working capacity. These are the most creative sources at a nation's disposal and upon them depends how far it is possible to exploit natural resources and productivity for the economic needs of man.

Natural resources other than agricultural are becoming more and more important in economic advancement. The first consideration would be that the area of arable land is not rigidly limited but is susceptible to change under the influence of artificial factors. Land is created through reclamation, drainage, terracing, irrigation, and so forth. The interchangeability of capital and land is produced by the application of capital to the soil. Further, development in the secondary and tertiary stages of production has little if any connection with population density.

The question arises whether inclusion of natural resources would provide a more exhaustive test of the capacity of a certain area to maintain its population. The following theoretical considerations bear on it:

> The conclusions reached from comparisons of population densities expressed in terms of natural resources have often been as misleading as those based on simple surface area density figures. The inadequacy of the population–natural-resources ratio derives from several causes. . . . Modern geographers are insisting that the resource today may be valueless tomorrow; what is valueless today may be a priceless resource a year hence. The only practical method of evaluating a resource is by its income-yielding capacity. . . . Only to the extent that a natural agent can be made to yield . . . [adequate returns to the capital and labor employed] may it properly be said to be a natural resource and can it be counted on to support population.[7]

Another objection is that some of the resources that gain

<hr />

[7] W. B. Hurd, "The Ability of Canada to Receive Immigration," quoted in H. F. Angus, "Canada and the Doctrine of Peaceful Change," in Wright, pp. 75, 76.

importance in the modern economic structure can never be quantitatively measured. The ones that matter most are skill and knowledge, capital funds, and the like.[8] The importance of capital equipment is growing.

The subjective qualities of the human material introduced into a certain territory are also an essential element in determining its absorptive capacity.[9] Such a factor as a "ferment of ideas" is certainly an imponderable that can never be taken into account in a static conception of economic absorption. The following seems to be true:

> . . . the economic forces determining the optimum location of industry and agriculture are changing. The natural properties of the soil, including access to waterways, are relatively less important; the quality of the population, and more particularly the ratio which the skilled and trained population bears to the whole, is becoming more important.[10]

The equilibrium of the components of an economy in their dynamic interaction, as well as technical culture and social relations such as distribution of wealth and income,

[8] Eugene Staley, *World Economy in Transition* (New York: Council on Foreign Relations, 1939), p. 292: "Natural resources are not by any means the only element in a country's ability to maintain a large population in comfort. Capital funds, making possible good industrial equipment, and intangible resources in knowledge and skill which raise the general level of productivity can be brought to the population more easily than the population can be moved to regions where these resources are already present."

[9] N. F. Hall, *Preliminary Investigation into Measures of a National or International Character for Raising the Standard of Living* (Geneva: Economic Committee, League of Nations, 1938), p. 48. "It is probable that one of the reasons why those countries which lie upon the principal channels of commerce have developed their economies relatively rapidly is to be found in that ferment of ideas which accompanies the intermingling of peoples and the interchange of commodities. In the absence of such interchanges of ideas, the mind cannot be quickened, traditional modes of life and of production are not subjected to critical scrutiny and the practical knowledge which is necessary before improved equipment can be used to increase efficiency does not develop. The potential productive capacity of the natural habitat is not realised and a vicious circle of ignorance and economic impotence results."

[10] *Ibid.*, p. 87.

affects the capacity of a country and a community to absorb an increment of population.

The utilization of available resources is at least as meaningful as their availability. A rise in productivity per man-day of labor would be the direct result of more intensive exploitation of productive resources. Some remarks of Mombert[11] are relevant. He holds that, wherever technique and economy have attained a certain degree of development, wherever population has reached a stage of cooperation and interaction, wherever growth of population stimulates a more thorough utilization of natural resources, the productivity of the individual rises with that growth. This takes place particularly in nations forced to side-step effects of the law of diminishing returns and to turn to lines of production in which a larger investment of capital and labor results in higher income. In that case, larger population frequently means higher productivity of capital.

On the other hand, occupational distribution and levels of development and standards of living in developed and underdeveloped countries, natural resources apart, appear to be correlated. The countries afflicted by problems of unemployment, underemployment, and low productivity (in farming especially) are those with a high proportion of their populations engaged in the primary stage of production. In developed countries, there is more division of labor, with its ancillary of rise in secondary and tertiary income, marking a changeover from production of goods to production of services. There, the accretion of capital equipment alters the economic structure in two respects: it superimposes an industrialized system of production on the developed economy; it raises the share of tertiary income by an ampler division of labor. The new population strata deposited by the accretion of capital and the structural transformation of the economy are the direct outcome of socio-economic changes, which

---

[11] Paul Mombert, *Grundriss der Sozialekonomik,* II Abteilung, "Wirtschaft und Bevoelkerung" (Tübingen: Verlag Mohr, 1914), p. 69.

react on the whole economy and speed the transition from a subsistence to an exchange economy.

Simon Kuznets has compiled long-period changes in the allocation of manpower for a large number of countries. In view of differences in the periods, it is not possible to make overall comparisons for developed and developing countries. His comparison for 1958 is shown in Table 2-3. Sixteen countries have been designated developed, and these have a minimum per capita GNP of $575. Fifteen countries have been designated intermediary, and they have a per capita GNP of $200–$574. Twelve countries designated less developed have a maximum per capita GNP of $199. Japan was included within the developed countries, despite its relatively low GNP per capita. The variance shown in the table has increased since 1958.

TABLE 2-3
Percentage of Labor Force, Excluding Unpaid Family Labor,
in the Three Stages of Production, 1958

Type of Country	Primary	Secondary	Tertiary
Developed	10.3	46.2	34.5
Intermediary	37.9	29.8	19.5
Less developed	57.6	19.5	22.9

Source: Simon Kuznets, *Modern Economic Growth: Rate, Structure and Spread* (New Haven, Conn.: Yale University Press), table 8.1.

This particular pattern of occupational distribution and the striking difference in this respect between developed and underdeveloped countries have repercussions on income distribution:

The situation is . . . complicated when income distribution within a population is very unequal and when it changes over time. This has been the case in many developing countries in recent years. In most of these countries nonfarm incomes are on the average much higher than farm incomes, often three times as high or even more. Because of the relatively slow increase in food production . . . farm incomes have on the whole been rising at very low annual rates, if at all. Now, if most of the income increase takes place in the small urban population where revenues are already relatively high, income elasticities calculated in the normal way become misleading because they assume that incomes increase evenly in the whole population.[12]

This situation is also reflected in Table 2-4, which shows the gap between agricultural and nonagricultural incomes in a number of countries that broadly represent the disparity between those occupied in primary and those in the secondary and tertiary stages of production.

The results of these conditions in underdeveloped countries are low productivity in the economy as a whole because

TABLE 2-4

Percentage of National Income per Worker in Agriculture
Compared with Other Branches of the Economy

Country	Percentage of agricultural workers among all workers		Percentage of national income from agriculture		Percentage of national income from nonagricultural activity
	Year	Per cent	Year	Per cent	
United Kingdom	1957	4.3	1957	4	93
Denmark	1953	23.6	1953	21	86
United States	1957	9.6	1957	5	60
Italy	1957	31.2	1957	20	55
Portugal	1950	48.4	1952	29	44
India	1951	70.6	1951	50	42
Canada	1957	15.5	1957	7	41
Japan	1957	39.3	1957	19	36
Yugoslavia	1953	66.0	1953	31	23
Mexico	1950	57.8	1950	20	18

Source: *Report of the Public Committee for the Investigation of the Situation of Agriculture in Israel* (Jerusalem, January, 1960), p. 25.

[12] OECD, *The Food Problem of Developing Countries* (Paris, 1968), p. 15.

of an imbalance between the primary and the secondary and tertiary stages of production, insufficient production of food by reason of low output in agriculture, incomes on or below subsistence level for large sections of the population, and a high rate of unemployment and underemployment. Too many people living off the land affect the economic structure and, first and foremost, the per capita rate of growth of the GNP.

On the face of it, the main economic objective of the Development Decade—a growth of the GNP in the developing countries by 5 per cent per annum—was nearly achieved, the actual figure in 1960–66 being 4.9 per cent. But this progress was adversely offset by the growth of population, which reduced the per head rise to 2 per cent. This fact has far-reaching economic consequences. It has been calculated that an average reduction in the rate of population growth in developing countries of one-tenth of 1 per cent could have a similar result as a rise of $600 million in capital formation.

In the developed world, the situation is totally different. There, the dynamics of development are based on a rapid shift from the primary to the secondary and tertiary stages of production, as Table 2-5 shows for the North Atlantic area (the United States, Canada, and western Europe). Overall statistics have been compiled for 1950 and 1960.

TABLE 2-5
Percentage Distribution of North Atlantic Area Labor Force
Among the Three Stages of Production

	Primary	*Secondary*	*Tertiary**	*Other†*
1950	21.6	34.6	39.5	4.3
1960	15.9	36.5	44.5	3.1
Per cent change	− 5.7	+ 1.9	+ 5.0	− 1.2

* Includes armed forces.
† Unemployed and other unclassified.

Source: Bernard Mueller, *A Statistical Handbook of the North Atlantic Area 1965* (The Twentieth Century Fund, 1965), table II-5.

For the United States, the long-period decline in the agricultural sector and the growth of the services sector are indicated in Table 2-6.

TABLE 2-6
Percentage Distribution of U.S. Labor Force Among
the Three Stages of Production

	Primary	*Secondary*	*Tertiary*
1870	43.7	27.1	25.6
1900	34.7	33.7	31.7
1930	21.9	35.8	42.3
1960	8.3	37.5	54.2

Source: OECD, *Manpower in the Service Sector, 1966* (Paris, 1967), table 3.

In the developed countries, manpower may become a factor limiting economic growth. The increment of manpower entering production is limited, and the danger of inflation is inseparable from an accelerated economic activity and an overheated economy. A minimum rate of frictional unemployment seems to be indispensable in restricting inflationary pressures, and, whenever overfull employment is reached, the rate of inflation is bound to distort the pattern of economic development and in the end to thwart economic growth.

These considerations prompted some developed countries in western Europe to import labor from southern Europe to cool the incandescent condition of their economies and curb inflationary pressures. Migration was mainly from southern Europe (southern Italy, Spain, Portugal, Greece, and, more recently, Turkey) to the industrialized north (West Germany, Belgium, Netherlands, Luxembourg, France, and Sweden), and to the former colonial powers from their quondam colonies—particularly from Algiers to France and from the colored Commonwealth to the United Kingdom. Inter-European migration was part of a general movement from rural to urban areas, accompanied by domestic migration within the more industrialized countries.

Among the few instances, the most impressive are those of West Germany, France, and Switzerland. There were about 950,000 foreign residents in West Germany in 1964, most of them from the Mediterranean basin. The quota of workers recruited abroad rose from 10,000 a year in the late 1950's, to 110,000 in 1960, to over 150,000 in 1961; these figures exclude people who originally came as tourists and found jobs.[13] France admitted some 53,000 Algerians in 1963 and as many in the first three months of 1964. There were some 1,800,000 foreign residents in France in 1962. Almost 30 per cent of the labor force in Switzerland is foreign, mainly Italian.[14]

The trends in the developed and in the underdeveloped countries seem to be contradictory. In the underdeveloped countries, there is a distinct surplus of unemployed or underemployed labor, particularly in the rural sector of the economy, and with this goes low productivity. In the developed countries, a shortage of labor and overfull employment seem to be the brake on economic growth. In the United States in 1960 there was a gap of some $50 billion between production potential and actual utilization, but this gap has nearly disappeared.

With the comparatively slow climb in population in the developed world, economic growth is chiefly the outcome of technological progress, but the steady expansion of the tertiary stage of production, which is influenced only peripherally by technological progress, tends to keep back the rise in production. Thus, opposite trends in retarding the speed of economic growth are involved: in the underdeveloped coun-

13 Charles Kindleberger, *Europe's Postwar Growth* (Cambridge, Mass.: Harvard University Press, 1967), pp. 176–77, 185–86.

14 *Ibid.*, pp. 175, 194, 211.

tries—population explosion, low productivity, low standards of life, and subsistence levels of income; in the developed countries—a slow increment of population and a shift to tertiary stages of production.

Total economic growth is determined by the productive factors that are in short supply, and, in the underdeveloped parts of the world, these are capital and skill. Accordingly, the problems of surplus population and of family planning present themselves as the main challenges of any economic policy intended to raise the standards of living and hasten economic growth. In the developed countries, shortage of manpower brakes that growth. The changeover from primary to secondary and tertiary stages of production cannot be avoided with the change in forms of consumption, which, as incomes go up, at a certain point expands more rapidly in the services than in the commodities sector. This structural alteration, as far as the tertiary stage is concerned, may affect the rate of economic growth.

In short, the underdeveloped nations suffer from malnutrition and insufficient food production, insufficient capital formation, unemployment, ignorance due to lack of education, and widespread disease—a cause of economic inefficiency. Shackled to that extent, they are unable to step up their production enough to overtake the per capita rates of growth of the developed nations.

Occupational distribution, as the complement of division of labor and a transition to modern types of economy, is an overriding factor in a country's capacity to carry a larger population. It reduces the importance of space and natural resources and gives a greater weight to other determinants of economic absorptive capacity. Economic development no longer squares with the primitive application of the Malthusian theory. The highest proportion of agricultural population is to be found in countries with the lowest standards of living, whereas progressive, yet still principally agricultural, economies such as Australia and New Zealand have a comparatively low percentage of it.[15] The explanation is higher productivity of labor and a switch to more up-to-date methods of farming.

The transfer from primary to secondary and tertiary stages of production is in most cases simultaneous with a rising standard of living, and this, with the accretion of capital equipment, subjects the economic structure to a twofold transformation. It superimposes an industrial system of production on the old economy, enlarges the share of tertiary income, consequent on greater division of labor, and it makes new openings of employment, which, in turn, bring the required labor force into being.

Diversified demand, the result of higher incomes, augments the share of secondary and tertiary stages of production. There must be fewer producers in the primary stage if their productivity is to rise, otherwise no market can be found for their products. The alternative is either many primary producers with low productivity, as in backward countries, or high productivity with fewer primary producers, as in the developed ones. The investigation by Klonov established that "a decline in the percentage of the agricultural population and an increase in the industrial population lead to an increase in the productivity of the soil and of agricultural labor,"[16] a process connected with the expansion of urban markets for farm produce.

The repercussions on both agricultural production and industrial concentration of a rise in population are favorable

---

15 Crocker, W. R.: "but one quarter of the Australian people are working on the land," Institute of Pacific Relations, *The Peopling of Australia,* Series No. 4 (Melbourne: Melbourne University Press, 1933), p. 134. See also pages 55, 56, 59, 109.

16 Klonov, *Recherches Statistiques sur la Relation entre la Productivité Agricole et la Densité et la Structure de la Population,* quoted in Imre Ferenczi, *The Synthetic Optimum of Population* (Paris: League of Nations, 1938), p. 31.

if the proportion of secondary and tertiary producers goes up.[17] In certain "colonization" countries, such developments were experienced gradually and slowly. The mechanism of them is described as follows:

> Even with improved technique, there are strict limits to the amount of fresh labour that can be employed without a decline in its reward, i.e., the standard of living. . . . This does not apply to the secondary industries, e.g., the finishing industry where land and other natural resources play a minor role compared with skill and organizing capacity and conditions of transport. If the supply of capital keeps pace with the increased quantity of labour, the output per head does not decline. On the contrary, it tends to increase with economies of large-scale production and industrial concentration. With the development of technical progress *per capita* production and the standard of living may even be subject to a rapid increase. That is what took place in all the industrial countries of Europe during the last half-century before the war, including those which acquired no colonies. The natural line of development for a nation whose population has reached a size at which returns in the primary industries tend to fall decisively is concentration on secondary industries. The output of vegetable agricultural products and of mineral raw materials will then absorb a decreasing proportion of the working population, while manufacturing industries, transportation and various services will employ an increasing proportion.[18]

Again the close link with markets is evident. The conclusion is obvious: for a country's ability to maintain a high standard of living or to raise it and to further economic growth,

[17] *The Peopling of Australia,* p. 117: "The natural capacity of secondary industries to maintain and absorb population depends not only on the resources available, but upon the extent to which the home market has become large enough to provide opportunities for large-scale production, and upon the use made of these opportunities. Natural growth is progressive and cumulative."

[18] Bert G. Ohlin, "Introductory Report on the Problem of International Economic Reconstruction," in Joint Committee of the Carnegie Endowment and of the International Chamber of Commerce, *International Economic Reconstruction: An Economist's and Businessman's Survey of the Main Problems of Today* (Paris: Development Center of the Organization of Economic Cooperation and Development), quoted in Wright, p. 288.

the relationship of population to such other, mainly mobile, resources as capital and skill is the determinant. The problem for underdeveloped countries is the procurement of mobile resources of skill, know-how, and, second to none, capital. Their growth potential is immense in view of the availability of surplus labor. The economies of scale, better interaction, and integration of population may, in certain circumstances, neutralize the higher density and actually become a factor promoting economic growth and even a per capita rise in the GNP.

In the past, as long as natural resources played a decisive part in economic progress, only migration movements could restore some equilibrium in economic conditions. Today, for social, ethnic, psychological, and political reasons, there is no possibility of any global redistribution of population, and escape from reliance on natural resources allows for the movement of resources to replace the movement of people. A copious supply of mobile resources of capital and skill opens up new avenues for raising agricultural productivity and for better utilizing unemployed and underemployed manpower through development of secondary and tertiary stages of production.

The present composition of populations in the underdeveloped countries, with an overwhelming proportion of them engaged in primary production, betrays a stage of underdevelopment. In the developed countries, the Keynesian idea of stimulation of economic growth by more intensive use of underutilized productive capacity has almost materialized. Global growth can, therefore, be fostered only by drawing the surplus manpower of underdeveloped countries, which constitutes an international labor reserve, into the process of world production. Thus, the population explosion may be considered a potential for new development, if there is an export of mobile resources to the underdeveloped areas of the world.

Poverty in the developed world has its core in maldistribution of income; in the underdeveloped world, in scarcity of
resources. In the developed world, it can be eliminated by
allocating a substantial proportion of the GNP to guarantee
a minimum or supplementary income. In the underdeveloped world, the provision of capital—including skill and education, entrepreneurial initiative, and effective demand—is
essential. In other words, the twin problems of strategy in the
war against poverty with which the world is faced are supply
of capital and effective demand.

However, this does not derogate from the appraisal made
by the President of the World Bank in October, 1968, that, in
existing circumstances:

> . . . the rapid growth of the population is one of the greatest
> barriers to the economic growth and social well-being of our
> member states. . . . Recent studies show the crippling effect
> of a high rate of population increase on economic growth in
> any developing country. For example, take two typical develop-
> ing countries with similar standards of living, each with a birth
> rate of 40 per 1,000 (this is the actual rate in India and Mexico),
> and estimate what would happen if the birth rate in one of
> those countries, in a period of 25 years, were to be halved to
> 20 per 1,000, a rate still well above that in most developed
> countries. The country which lowered its population growth
> would raise its standard of living 40 per cent above the other
> country in a single generation.
>
> In terms of the gap between rich countries and poor, these
> studies show that more than anything else it is the population
> explosion which, by holding back the advancement of the
> poor, is blowing apart the rich and the poor and widening the
> already dangerous gap between them.

It is evident that the population-land ratio cannot be a
valid criterion of economic capacity to support a rising population and, furthermore, that effective demand of a rising
population is an agent of economic growth. The question,
then, must be asked whether and why family planning and

population control are desirable and even indispensable aspects of any economic policy aiming at the abolition of poverty.

There are three main reasons for the policy of restricting excessive proliferation of populations. First, a projection into the next century, taking present rates of increment, shows an overall population density on the globe comparable with the most populous countries of today. That development would bring with it a further and dangerous rise in air and water pollution, conurbations with substandard housing, education, and public amenities, and other unwelcome adjuncts of overconcentrations of population. The prospects for social and cultural amelioration to come would be of the darkest.

A resolution sponsored by fifty-six members of the United Nations and adopted by the General Assembly on December 31, 1968, points out that, because of modern scientific and technological developments, the relationship between man and his environment is in the process of undergoing profound changes and that, unless these changes are "properly controlled," the consequences will "involve grave dangers" for mankind. The resolution notes "the continuing and accelerating impairment of the quality of the human environment caused by such factors as air and water pollution, erosion and other forms of soil deterioration, waste, noise and secondary effects of biocides, which are accentuated by rapidly increasing population and accelerating urbanization." Referring to the developing countries, the resolution expresses the strong hope that they, through appropriate channels of international cooperation, will "derive particular benefit from the mobilization of knowledge and experience about the problems of human environment, enabling them, *inter alia,* to forestall the occurrence of many such problems."

Second, economic growth per head and capital formation would be slowed down and gravely handicapped by the need to provide the vast new excess of population with agricultural and industrial capacity of production and with transport, as well as schools, hospitals, and other benefits.

Third, the advantages of an economy of growing population presuppose a growing effective demand. There is, however, no chance that capital provided to the underdeveloped world would suffice both to finance and facilitate expansion of productive capacity and also to raise standards of consumption appreciably. Even with a substantially limited natural increase, brought down to the rate prevailing in developed countries, this would be a herculean task, considering the enormous discrepancy in standards of consumption and productive capacity between the two parts of the world. If present rates of natural increase persist, the whole process of economic growth and rising standards will be undone. That being so, the case for an economy of growing population with expanding effective demand in no way contradicts the case for limiting excessive rises in population. It aims, rather, at financing a rise in the effective demand of a population growing more restrainedly.

Granted that the rigid formula of relationship between natural resources and population is unrealistic, there is an economic natural limit to a too rapid rise in population. Oversight of this limit would tend to retard economic growth and capital formation. It follows that, notwithstanding the theoretical merits of an economy of growing population, a dual approach is imperative, circumscribing natural increase by family planning and endowing the population of underdeveloped countries with immensely larger resources of capital and skill. There is no probability of a transfer of mobile resources on the phenomenal scale that present rates of natural increase require, nor is there the capacity to absorb such an inundation of mobile resources within a reasonable time.

Recent projections reveal that investment in population control is probably the most effective and growth-stimulating use of resources in developing countries. The use of resources for this purpose is limited because of social and psychological constraints. However, the control of population growth in developing countries could, in the long run, change the ratio of population to capital stock at their disposal and thus increase productivity and per capita incomes, as capital equipment per capita is augmented by the slowing down of the rate of natural increase. This would be of particular importance and effectiveness in promoting economic growth in developing countries with large-scale unemployment and underemployment.

Quantitative limitation would improve the quality of the population thanks to rising nutritional standards and more extensive educational facilities. As a result of population control, higher incomes and a higher rate of saving would be conducive to a more rapid internal accumulation of capital.

Model projections for different underdeveloped countries reflect similar positive effects of declining fertility on economic growth and on total and per capita national incomes. The present maldistribution of population and capital is such that, without birth control and family planning, even an accelerated tempo of transfer of mobile resources to the underdeveloped parts of the world could not cure their economic troubles. Global demographic development does not hold out any prospect of solving economic problems unless population is controlled:

It took the world over 18 centuries to increase its population from a quarter to one billion persons. Today one billion persons are being added every 15 years, and the world population is growing at a rate that is 30 times as high as the average rate of growth between the first century A.D. and 1650. In less developed countries that rate is 40 times as high.[19]

No speed or scope of economic advance can match so ungoverned an explosion of new lives.

[19] George C. Zaidan, "Population Growth and Economic Development," *Finance and Development,* Vol. 6 (Washington, D.C.: March, 1969).

3 Capital

Of mobile resources, the most important is capital. It is the key to the solution of the problem of how to expand productive equipment and productive capacity to match a growing population. Only if capital equipment—industrial and agricultural machinery, pipes, water-boring machinery, and the like—expands per capita and not in the aggregate alone and an equilibrium is established between accretion of productive equipment and the demographic increment, can it be assumed that economic growth has been instrumental in raising standards of living and enlarging productivity.

The population explosion postulates higher productive capacity and more equipment; that is a precondition of economic absorption of the demographic increment. So, one of the vital prerequisites of development is capital equipment. It makes for expansion of production, industrialization, and occupational redistribution, for it is a truism that "lack of capital and of capital equipment is one of the causes of Eastern poverty, and of the greatest obstacles to industrial development."[1] Accordingly, a certain relation between accretion of capital, demographic increment, and the average unit per capita of capital will adjust the level of economic activity and the standard of living. The relevance of this calculation is to be seen in the following definitions:

[1] Harold Butler, *Problems of Industry in the East, with Special Reference to India, French India, Ceylon, Malaya, and the Netherlands Indies* (Geneva: International Labour Office, 1938), p. 73.

. . . the ability of a country to sustain an increase in population depends not only upon the wealth of its natural resources, but also upon its capital equipment and upon the technical ability of its producers. For this reason, a relatively undeveloped country may give signs of a temporary rural overpopulation in spite of rich natural resources, if the rate of growth of its population is more rapid than the growth of its capital equipment and the development of its industrial and agricultural technique.

A large number of the countries with rapidly increasing population are agricultural and lack capital. Such countries may be faced with serious economic problems as their population growth leads to rural overpopulation. . . . Even if they possess raw materials, lack of capital may prevent them from exploiting these resources and from industrialising; for their own savings will probably be meagre and it will be difficult for them to borrow from abroad.[2]

With populations rising so rapidly, capital accumulation could not be swift enough to expand productive factors at a corresponding tempo. It requires the spur of an external source of capital, lent or invested.

The more population, the less the available per capita space and natural resources. On the other hand, this inversion can be offset to some extent by an increment of available capital equipment per inhabitant. A survey of natural resources will not yield enough material for estimates of absorptive capacity, for those resources only represent potentiality, and their utilization largely depends upon there being adequate capital equipment. The effect of these conflicting and divergent factors on the approach of the population to a hypothetical optimum turns not a little on their quantitative relations and interaction. The standard of living and the national income may serve here as indicators. Thus, the requirement of Mombert is that, "at the present stage of economic development the necessary preliminary condition for the absorptive capacity of an economy to keep pace with the

---

2 League of Nations, *World Economic Survey, 1938–39*, p. 159.

increase of population is the yearly provision of new capital goods in such quantities as to correspond at least to the average per capita of the existing population."[3] There is also the effect of transition to a capital-intensive economy on occupational distribution.

More capital equipment should lead to a greater division of labor and simplify the passage to modern forms of economy. Of that transformation the accompaniment is a crossing from production of goods to production of services, preceded by a process of industrialization making availability of capital an imperative prerequisite of such industrialization. If the degree of utilization of existing resources, natural and human, is to make up for their scarcity, a full stock of capital in the form of capital goods is essential.

Interchangeability of capital, space, and other assets is decisively important, particularly as there is a certain degree of correlation between capital investment and productivity. Clearly, the development of an area depends on the supply of capital.

Another *sine qua non* of the successful absorption of a growing population is intake of skill, know-how, and training, which affect the population's quality. How significant this intake is the following shows:

> Large fixed investments are represented in the special skills of the expert shoemaker, the designers of women's fashions, the mining engineer, the industrial chemist, the expert farmer, the marine navigator, the bone surgeon, the maker of optical goods, the jewel cutter, the horticulturalist, the architect of bridges, the irrigation engineer. . . . Finally, there is a human resource not entirely bound to any particular persons but socially carried, and institutionally preserved and fostered: knowledge, especially the systematic knowledge of science, and industrial techniques based upon it. This resource exists in libraries, in laboratories, in universities and public school sys-

[3] Paul Mombert, *Grundriss der Sozialekonomik,* II Abteilung, "Wirtschaft und Bevoelkerung" (Tübingen: Verlag Mohr, 1914), p. 79.

tems, in the practices of office and shop and mill, in the tradi-
tions of science and scientific spirit.

Important parts of it are the "atmosphere" of a particular
culture. Knowledge of different kinds, techniques of different
kinds, are unevenly distributed over the earth today and probably always will be, despite rapid communication, because
knowledge is highly specialized.[4]

With more and more emancipation from natural conditions
and a greater weight of the knowledge factor, of organizing
ability, and so forth, this aspect exerts a stronger influence.

The connection between the greater availability of capital
equipment and economic growth is attested by the correlation between economic growth in underdeveloped countries
where the pace of it is significant and the injection of capital.
A study by the OECD, *Population Control and Economic
Development,* confirms this, particularly as regards the integration of modern technology in the economic growth pattern of underdeveloped countries:

> To focus on capital seems warranted even if, in a broad view
> of the obstacles to development, innumerable other factors
> compete for attention; above all, perhaps, administrative and
> institutional problems, and foreign exchange difficulties. It is,
> nevertheless, in terms of capital shortage that development
> planners most acutely experience the difficulty of "embodying"
> modern technology.[5]

Capital supply, therefore, is the crucial problem for the developing parts of the world.

The industrialized, developed economy of the West was
built on formation of capital by a ruthless lowering of the
standards of living of large sections of the population in the
eighteenth and nineteenth centuries. That solution does not

---

4 Eugene Staley, *World Economy in Transition* (New York: Council on
Foreign Relations, 1939), p. 73.

5 Goran Ohlin, *Population Control and Economic Development* (Paris:
Development Center of the Organization of Economic Cooperation and Development, 1967), p. 56.

offer itself comparably to the underdeveloped nations because their minimum subsistence level, just keeping body
and soul together, is already so low that not much more can
be extracted for investment. Moreover, modern technology
magnifies the capital requirements for investment. And, even
now, some 80 per cent of all capital formation in underdeveloped countries is derived from internal sources of saving
and accumulation of capital. In other words, some four-fifths
of investment there is resources wrung out of populations
living on or below subsistence levels. Even this apparently
positive development is not an unmixed blessing, for it implies a reduction in consumption of local products, capital
goods as a rule being imported. Paradoxical as it may sound,
in the underdeveloped world it is almost as important to
finance primary consumption as it is to finance development.
The main driving force for any stepping-up of production is
a larger market. At the outset of development, higher consumption elicits demand and allows for the establishment of
many an enterprise whose feasibility is predicated on economies of scale. The experience of countries that are presented
as "success stories" teaches that their development was based
above all else on effective demand, on which are founded
their economies of scale in numerous industries. Besides,
rising levels of consumption prompt a rise in productivity
and efficiency through the medium of higher standards of
nutrition and education.

In the eighteenth and nineteenth centuries, there was no
alternative in the West to internal formation of capital. Today, an alternative exists—the simple device of transfer. The
difficulty of primary accumulation of capital was virtually
overcome by transfer of capital from more developed countries—in such new areas as the United States, Canada, and
Australia—and the resources are equally available now. The
periodic recessions in the developed economies affect, in the
main, industries producing capital goods and contract their

output to four or five times below that of other industries. A transfer of capital to underdeveloped countries, particularly in such periods, would help to iron out the unevennesses of boom and slump in the industrialized world.

At the present moment, this transfer is static at some $10 billion to $11 billion net a year. This is practically retrogression, considering the rapid population rise in the developing countries, which reduces the capital transferred per head, and considering also the secular drop in prices of primary products side by side with the mounting prices of capital goods and industrial products, which erode the real value of the transfers. The amount of capital will dwindle under present conditions, because the burden of debt repayments becomes enormous by reason of the devastating effect of compound interest on long-term loans.

Moreover, most of this flow of capital is based on bilateral agreements and tied to definite sources of supply, and thus its effectiveness is reduced as the recipient country is deprived of the advantages of competitive bidding. The quality and price of goods are in these cases determined by the monopolistic control of the country, which provides by grants or credit the financial means for the purchase of goods.

The diminution of aid, with a reversal in the 1960's of the trend of the 1950's to pour capital more lavishly into the underdeveloped world, tells a sad and sorry tale. The sum of capital transferred from the developed to the underdeveloped two-thirds of mankind is being whittled away by poorer terms of trade and by the population explosion. Relatively, the erosion is even more pronounced, for the net flow of capital is today slightly more than one half of 1 per cent of the GNP of $1,850 billion from a rapidly swelling volume of production in the developed countries. Moreover, the more than eightfold gap in per capita investment between the privileged and the underprivileged parts of the world foreshadows an even gloomier future.

At the present rate of the flow of capital, as a share that is becoming smaller and smaller of a GNP in the developed countries that is becoming bigger and bigger, any approach to a more acceptable economic relationship between the two divisions of mankind would take centuries to yield results. In the late 1960's, the flow has almost come to a point of stagnation.

The share of grants in official bilateral aid has declined from 75 per cent in 1961 to 65 per cent in 1965, 63 per cent in 1966, and 59 per cent in 1967.[6] The 1966 report of the IMF mentions that the growth in the transfer of capital to developing countries in the period 1960–65 was less than in the five previous years and that "the growth of per capita output was distinctly lower than in the second half of the 1950's." Thus, the gaps between the developed and the under-developed parts of the world, one in standards and consumption and the second, even more perilous and portentous, in investment, may bring us to the brink of failure if the scope and conditions of aid are frozen in their present dimensions.

The terms and stipulations of loans are certainly no less important than the scope of aid. The same report of the World Bank says: "Between 1962 and 1966, payments of amortization and interest on external public debt grew at an average annual rate of 10 per cent, considerably faster than the increase in exports of goods and services by developing countries as a group." The debt service of ninety-two developing countries aggregated some $3,900 million in 1966. The cumulative onus of debts is a sort of time bomb, which may burst at any moment in the 1970's, when debt repayments will amount to as much as the entire financial help. The accumulated debt of ninety-two underdeveloped countries increased fourfold in one decade—1956 to 1967.

During 1967, there was a deterioration in the overall terms

[6] See the 1966 annual reports of the IBRD and the IMF (Washington, D.C., 1967).

of development finance. For DAC member countries as a whole, grants as a percentage of total commitments fell from approximately 60 per cent in 1966 to 55 per cent in 1967. Weighted average interest rates on official bilateral commitments rose from 3.1 per cent in 1965 to 3.8 per cent in 1967.

According to study made by the UNCTAD Secretariat entitled *Trends and Problems in World Trade and Development: Growth, Development Finance and Aid Synchronization and National Policies* (Doc. TD. 34), debt service payments will account for almost 80 per cent of the projected trade gap for 1975 on the low growth assumption and for about 60 per cent on the high growth assumption. They surpass in both cases the current net capital flows to developing countries and represent 18 and 19 per cent respectively of projected exports, as against 13 per cent of exports in 1963. These are the average figures for all developing countries. For part of them, the debt service ratio to exports was much higher, as we know from the special analysis of debt servicing of twenty-four countries. Furthermore, debt service payments of the developing countries amounted in 1963, according to the same source, to about $4.9 billion, more than half of the net capital inflow in that year, which totaled $9.5 billion.

The dark forebodings about the conditions of aid have been more than justified, especially where the evaluation of conventional but unrealistic, instead of concessionary, terms of lending is in question. The developed world is deluding itself by the new expedient of rescheduling debts, which is merely make-believe. The loans are contracted on conventional terms, and the fiction of respectability is duly acknowledged. In lieu of concessionary terms at the outset, the less desirable stratagem is used of changing the conditions *post factum*, with unfavorable effects on the credit standing of the debtor countries.

One of the illusions that must be dispelled in this connection is that the problem of the underdeveloped world can be solved by private investment. The report of the Development Assistance Committee of the OECD says this: "Unfortunately, it appears that the increase in official net disbursements was more than offset by a reduction in private investment. This decline has taken place despite increased efforts by governments in various developed countries to encourage foreign investment."

Private capital is not attracted to investment in underdeveloped countries because of low profitability, shortage of skilled labor, lack of scientific facilities, limited internal markets, and higher risk. In the circumstances, government and international economic aid becomes a cardinal means of transferring capital to them from developed countries; yet transfer, whether measured by the needs or by the capacity of the transferors, is actually falling away.

The World Bank calculates the capacity of developing countries to absorb investments productively and usefully at $3 billion to $4 billion per annum over and above the present volume of capital transfers. As far as transfer-capacity of the developed world is concerned, the following figures of the proportion of economic aid within its GNP are illuminating. Out of a GNP of at least $1,850 billion in 1967, the net amount assigned to the progress of underdeveloped countries was $11.6 billion or 0.6 per cent, and much of that amount consists of commercial credits such as financing of exports and other similar short-term devices.

The atrophy of aid to underdeveloped countries, calculated as a share of the GNP of the developed world, testifies to frustration, futility, and failure in this crucial epoch of human endeavor. In 1962, that form of succor constituted 0.76 per cent of the GNP of the developed world; in 1963, it fell to 0.70 per cent; in 1964, to 0.69 per cent; and in 1966, to as little as 0.62 per cent, after a short-lived recovery to 0.72 per cent in 1965.

Where is the capital to come from to solve this ever acute

problem? Internal formation of capital is necessarily limited by the low level of per capita income in underdeveloped countries, and it would be intolerable, in present conditions, to virtually squeeze every ounce of possible savings from their undernourished peoples when the developed world enjoys immense increments of GNP, some $80 billion every year.

Capital is, of course, raised domestically in developing countries up to four-fifths of the total investment; but it must be supplemented to a much greater degree than it now is by transfer of financial resources from the developed world, particularly with modern technology—demanding investment of large sums—and, be that transfer ever so massive, development is still a long and steep and arduous trek.

However, it is a reassuring fact that, wherever capital was available, the results pleased. To quote a report on research carried out for the Office of Program Coordination of AID:

> The possibilities of securing rapid and sustained development by effective use of foreign assistance have been strikingly demonstrated in the past decade by such countries as Greece, Israel, Taiwan, and the Philippines. In each case, a substantial increase in investment financed largely by foreign loans and grants has led to rapid growth of GNP followed by a steady decline in the dependence on external financing. Not only was growth accelerated by foreign assistance, but the ability of each economy to sustain further development from its own resources was very substantially increased.

Most of the countries—Iran, Israel, Korea, Malaysia, Mexico, Pakistan, Taiwan, Thailand, Tunisia, Venezuela, and Yugoslavia among them—that were catalogued at the 1967 meeting of the board of governors of the World Bank by President Woods as exemplifying success in economic growth are incontrovertible demonstrations that investment, although not the only condition, is one of the chief prerequisites of development.

The ebbing of capital flow to underdeveloped countries as a share of the GNP of the developed world is bound to be accelerated by debt explosion; already about half of the financial aid given to underdeveloped countries is swallowed up by repayment of the principal and interest of their debts, and some time in the 1970's will be the calamitous zero hour when that repayment comes to as much as the rate of assistance to them, unless their infusion of capital is greater. They are practically saturated with credit on commercial terms, even World Bank terms. Their credit-worthiness is jeopardized by the burden of indebtedness and may be further impaired if rescheduling is practiced. There can be but one conclusion: grants or concessionary advances alone can avert total invalidation of aid. More, not less, investment must be forthcoming if the developing world is ever to catch up. The yearly net capital investment per head is $354 in the developed and $42 in the developing states, a ratio of 1 : 8.5, whose continuance no one can contemplate with equanimity. Investment, however, depends largely on capital flow, and economic growth is, not inconsiderably, the function of investment.

A new myth, a new kind of escapism, is currently circulated: growth is so overwhelmingly a function of knowledge and technological level that there is no point in spilling capital into countries lacking those virtues. However, the truth is that technical assistance is more readily procurable than capital is. U.N. technical assistance, the OECD, and bilateral technical aid are at gratuitous disposal, and more can be purchased on the free market, so that there is a considerable availability.

It would, of course, be wrong to decry the value of technical aid, but it should not be used today as a substitute for the flow of capital or as an excuse for slowing it down. The fact that it requires less capital is in its favor as a developmental stimulant. Within five years, technical aid has grown by some 50 per cent but capital transfer by only 8 per cent. It must not, however, become just a means of relieving and lightening the guilt complex of the developed world. Not that it can be claimed that capital alone suffices; however, it is indispensable, and, if it fails to flow, other aids will not avail. Capital transfer is, indisputably, the central problem in the economic growth of the developing world, and the disparity between the demand for capital and its supply doubtless reflects a present direction of flow at variance with man's global needs and contrary to what those needs predicate as desirable.

The IMF reports that the flow of capital to developing countries in the period 1960–65 expanded less than in the previous quinquennium and that "the growth of per capita output was distinctly lower than in the second half of the 1950's." This flow of capital consists of three elements: grants-in-aid, private investment, and capital markets.

Grants-in-aid, as a share of the total flow of capital, decreased from 76 per cent in 1961 to 55 per cent in 1967 of a total that did not increase substantially. Present experience of budgetary allocations points to a virtual impossibility of any substantial addition to aid by the simple system of state grants. Not even the World Bank or any similar institution could annually secure a billion or more dollars from such grants, which, to start with, have to be accorded precedence inside the political pattern of democracy.

Private investment aggregated $4.1 billion in 1965 and $4.2 billion in 1967, again reflecting almost complete stagnation. Moreover, this flow of private investment was, to an overwhelming degree, directed to certain branches of economy in a few countries—predominantly the exploitation of oil resources.

The one source resorted to, to a very small extent, is the capital market. The share of underdeveloped nations in international issues was negligible, and the capital markets were utilized for development of less developed countries almost exclusively through the issues of World Bank bonds.

We have here a clear-cut case for priorities. Some $39 billion of domestic fixed-interest securities were launched on the world's capital markets in 1966 (of which some $3 billion were international and foreign securities), and some $41 billion in 1967. According to a report by UNCTAD's Secretariat: "during the period 1960–66, there has been a substantial increase in the volume of net issues by both the public and private sectors of these countries. Public and private borrowing on a net basis rose from approximately $16.7 billion in 1960 to $39.2 billion in 1966." The share of developing countries in that colossal accumulation of capital is microscopic and confined to two or three countries with special conditions.

The Economic and Social Council of the United Nations comments thus on the problem:

> The developing countries have relatively little access to the world's capital markets. This is in part a problem of regulations and procedures but at root it reflects the inadequacy of their credit standing when judged by market criteria. In recent years, moreover, conditions have been particularly tight in most markets, and interest rates appreciably higher than those at which the developing countries have in fact borrowed from governments and from international institutions. If, in order to avoid the budgetary constraint and to take advantage of favourable balance of payments positions in particular countries, more use is to be made of the capital market, it will thus have to be done through a mechanism which has both an appropriate credit ranking and the ability to re-lend at less than market rates.

This, verily, is the crux: access of developing countries to the free capital market.

The 1967 review of the OECD, *Development Assistance, Efforts and Policies,* puts the case in unequivocal and impressive terms:

The problem for the Member of DAC is essentially one of the degree of priority which is being given to aid. Governments may consider as obstacles to increases of assistance such conditions as balance of payments difficulties, fear of overheating the economy with resultant inflation, and budgetary limitations. The last item is merely a polite way of saying that domestic claims such as roadbuilding, agricultural support, defence, space exploration, or more generous social security scales take priority. Of course, one should not set these various objectives one against the other. The choices which underlie budgetary decisions are not made in terms of absolute priority but of shifts at the margin. And a slight marginal shift in some larger budgetary areas could provide quite substantial increases in aid resources. The problem for countries wishing to provide assistance is also, like that of the recipients, essentially political.

It cannot be contended that a 1 per cent allocation from a GNP of some \$1,850 billion in 1967 would be onerous for the developed world, which is getting richer year after year, yet it would nearly double the capital flow of that twelve-month period, and that, surely, is far from crying for the moon. The difficulties of the balance of payments, too, could be resolved by some such method as suggested by the President of the World Bank respecting IDA replenishment—a method that would provide for a coordination of the use of the equivalent of sales of bonds in the various countries with purchases in their markets, if those difficulties were to necessitate it. This would avoid the pitfalls and shortcomings of tied aid, for it would apply to timing only; repercussions of that form of aid on prices and terms would be prevented. The World Bank and other institutions cannot do without access to the capital markets of the world if they are to work for the good of progress in the underprivileged sector of mankind.

That sector is barred from such access by lack of security and by high interest rates beyond its capacity to pay, a capacity even more clipped in recent years by a rise in those rates.

Among the arguments against providing for access to the capital markets by developing countries are the tightness of those markets and the high cost of money. But this is a double-edged sword and cuts both ways, making it more mandatory than ever to furnish special easements to developing states. Otherwise, they have not the remotest chance of raising funds of the magnitude required.

This is primarily a question of priorities. It is not credible that every one of the annual flotations of $40 billion of internal and external issues on the capital markets of the world today has, from the global angle, absolute precedence over the needs of underdeveloped countries.

One possible way of overcoming the obstacles of access of developing nations to capital markets is the application of the so-called Horowitz Proposal, accurately summarized in the report of UNCTAD's Secretariat:

> The proposal rests on the generally accepted premise that the flow of aid to developing countries needs to be greatly increased and that the terms of assistance have to be softened considerably so as to permit an adequate net transfer of resources to developing countries and also to prevent explosive debt situations from emerging. It further assumes that, because of budgetary contraints, there are limits to the growth of official aid flows but that requisite resources for aid can be found in the capital markets of the developed countries. Since funds on the capital markets can only be raised on commercial terms, there is need for subsidies to make these funds available on soft terms to developing countries. Thus, the proposal envisages an international institution raising funds on national capital markets of developed countries on normal commercial terms and relending these funds through the IDA to developing countries at low rates of interest for a suggested period of thirty years.[7] The difference between the cost of borrowing to the institution and the lower rates of interest on lending

[7] The international institution concerned could be the World Bank or the IDA itself. The funds raised would be additional to those required by the Bank for its normal transactions, and the resulting obligations would be backed by new and independent guarantees.

would be covered by an interest equalization fund. The resources for this fund would be obtained through budgetary allocations of the developed countries to the IDA, through the allocation of some portion of net income of the World Bank, or through some combination of both methods.

The proposal was adopted in its entirety, to all intents and purposes, in Algiers by the seventy-seven nations and is incorporated in the Algiers Charter in Chapter C, "Development Financing," paragraphs 2(b), (c), and (d), under the name of the Multilateral Interest Equalization Fund.

The report on the proposal prepared by UNCTAD's Secretariat testified eloquently to the possibilities inherent in it:

32. If restrictions on national capital markets are eased or eliminated in the longer run, it would appear that there should be ample scope for schemes of the type discussed in this report. Both the interest equalization fund and the institution of an appropriate system of guarantees present no serious technical problems. It is now generally recognized that there is a need to improve the functioning of capital markets in order to facilitate and to increase the transfer of savings into long-term investment. If such improvements take place, and if the vast institutional savings which flow into capital markets continue their annual rates of increase, it would be reasonable to assume that significant amounts of resources could be raised for re-lending to developing countries at low rates of interest.

It is worthy of mention that the high-level Perkins Committee recommended a study of the proposal as follows:

7. *Innovations for the Longer Term*

. . .

Another possibility would be to finance at least part of a future IDA replenishment through government commitments to subsidize interest payments on IDA bonds sold in private capital markets. This would lessen the burden of replenishment on member country budgets, and thus might permit a substantially larger replenishment than would otherwise be negotiable. If, for example, a government undertook to provide an additional $100 million a year for ten years in this manner and to reimburse IDA for six per cent a year on the amount borrowed, the budgetary burden would grow gradually from $6 million in the first year to $60 million in the tenth and succeeding years. If this were done prudently, expanding capital markets ought to be able to absorb both new issues and reissues of such securities.

In an opening statement of the UNCTAD Secretariat, the situation with regard to the Horowitz Proposal is defined as follows:

> At the technical level the proposal has been examined most thoroughly and carefully by the staff of the World Bank, by an UNCTAD expert group, and by the UNCTAD Secretariat. All three studies make it quite clear that the proposal is technically feasible, but that it raises policy issues which only governments can decide.

Analysis of the capital markets affords evidence that, on the basis of priority, they should be capable of allocating some share of the amounts raised by fixed-interest bonds to fertilize the growth of developing countries.

Total public and private borrowing on a net basis in the domestic capital markets of the developed countries rose from approximately $16.7 billion in 1960 to $39.2 billion in 1966 and to $41 billion in 1967. Net foreign issues on national markets rose from approximately $0.8 billion in 1960 to $1.9 billion in 1966. Moreover, in 1968 there was a further spectacular increase in international bond loans, reaching the amount of $4.7 billion, doubling the relatively high 1967 level.

The report by UNCTAD's Secretariat comments on this point:

> 21. The foregoing account makes it clear that during the 1960's there has been significant growth in the capital markets of developed countries. It is of course true that many of these

markets have been faced in recent years with tight conditions. But this is because the demand for long-term funds has increased even faster than the supply. However, the tightness of markets has not always been due to the shortage of savings. As a recent EEC report has pointed out, "The present shortcomings of the capital markets are not due so much to insufficient savings as to the impossibility of adjusting correctly supply and demand on markets that are too narrow."[8]

Further, a study prepared by R. N. Cooper and E. M. Truman of Yale University, entrusted by the Secretary-General of UNCTAD with the task of analyzing capital markets particularly in relation to underdeveloped nations, includes the following comments:

1. The need of developing countries for capital from abroad is a continuing one. Efforts to increase the flow of economic assistance have been very successful in a number of donor countries, but several major donor countries have retrenched and are engaged in an extensive re-evaluation of their aid programs. Thus, while the need grows, the prospect of meeting the need from normal channels of foreign assistance fades.

2. At the same time, international capital markets have shown a revival in activity reminiscent of the 1920's. This revival raises the possibility that developing countries may rely more heavily on international bond issues in private markets as a source of foreign funds. . . .

4. . . . During the 1960's foreign bond issues have grown very rapidly, both in New York and in the new international bond, or Eurobond, market in Europe; in 1968 they exceeded $5 billion in value. Increasing numbers of developing countries have floated foreign issues, with the total aggregating nearly $500 million in 1967; and the World Bank and the Inter-American Development Bank have each raised large sums on capital markets, to be re-lent to developing countries.

.   .   .

[8] EEC Commission, *Development of a European Capital Market,* report of a group of experts appointed by the Commission (November, 1966), p. 15.

Easing the Terms of Borrowing on Capital Markets

102. The problem of debt servicing can be eased by lengthening the maturities and reducing the interest rates on the external debt of the developing countries. Foreign assistance by the donor nations is the principal means employed at present to ease these terms. Although flotations on private capital markets must be competitive in the eyes of the bond-holder with alternative uses for his funds, there are several ways in which private capital can be raised on terms less onerous to the borrowing countries than at present.

103. The most frequently discussed proposal is one put forward at the first UNCTAD session in 1964 by David Horowitz of the Bank of Israel. The Horowitz proposal would involve IDA borrowing on the major capital markets, of IBRD borrowing on behalf of IDA, for relending to developing countries at the easy terms associated with IDA loans. These bonds would be guaranteed by donor nations. The difference between IDA borrowing costs and its receipts from lending would be made up by an "interest equalization fund" subscribed by the developed countries. Thus the difference between borrowing costs of, say, $6\frac{1}{2}$ per cent and IDA's charge of $\frac{3}{4}$ per cent—$5\frac{3}{4}$ per cent—would be a grant by the donor countries. The thought underlying this proposal is that far more capital could be mobilized for developing countries in this way than if sole or principal reliance were placed on foreign aid appropriations by the donor countries; a dollar's appropriation could be used to stimulate several dollars' worth of private lending. It should be noted, however, that some adjustment might also be required to match the maturities of IDA/IBRD borrowing—long-term international bond issues rarely exceed 25 years—and the typical 50 year maturity of IDA loans.

All that, of course, provided the flow of capital to developing countries is not considered only residual, after all other needs, more or less urgent, have been satisfied.

It is decidedly preferable to enable the developing countries to buy money on the market on conditions compatible with their capacity to repay, rather than rely entirely on taxation to provide the necessary capital. It is illusory to suppose that, in a democracy, taxation yielding enough for aid to other nations is a realistic concept; experience of the extent of capital flow to developing countries and of IDA replenishment in particular is the proof. Money is always available at a price, if the proper collateral and interest are forthcoming. The Horowitz Proposal is meant to build a bridge of collateral and concessionary terms for the borrower and a reasonable yield for the lender by making it possible to borrow hard and lend soft. Under present conditions, even the exemption from interest equalization tax extended by the U.S. government to developing countries on the U.S. capital markets could not be utilized, and only two such countries were able to make their way in, favored by specially and virtually unique circumstances.

The important point of the Horowitz Proposal is not only the alleviation of the terms of aid, but also—possibly even to a greater extent—the promotion of a larger flow of loan capital to the underdeveloped nations. Obviously, with the interest subsidy, the constraint and limitations imposed by the price of money on the capital markets are reduced, and greater flexibility in meeting the commercial terms of capital is conferred on the international institutions, such as the World Bank and the regional development banks.

The interest subsidy should always be calculated in relation to the amount raised in one year, as the source of the subsidy would always have to be recurrent, through budgetary and other allocations. Moreover, for each billion dollars, the annual amount of the interest subsidy is the same, but from the economic point of view it must be taken into account that it has to be drawn each year from an increasing GNP and expanding budgets of the developed nations and is therefore relatively declining.

One of the arguments raised is that the amount for a number of years is so large that the benefit accruing from this method is not worth the price. The point of departure for this assumption is the erroneous illusion that otherwise the price is not paid. The price, which is the annual interest, is being paid anyhow. The difference is that in case of the application of the Horowitz plan the amount is paid to the citizens of the country that lends the money to the underdeveloped country, with no implications for the balance of payments and a reduced burden for the treasury because income from bonds is taxable, while without the application of the Horowitz plan the same payment is made by transfer of resources from the underdeveloped (borrowing) to the developed (lending) country. Thus, the illusion must be dispelled that the Horowitz plan imposes a burden of payment of interest, which otherwise does not exist. Evidently, it is only a shift from the underdeveloped to the developed country, without any additional burden on the latter, from the point of view of the balance of payments, as the interest is paid to the citizens of the developed country. Of course, in this case the developed country foregoes an addition to its foreign currency by transfer of interest payments from the underdeveloped country. The economic justification of such a shift from the point of view of development and the general philosophy of the World Bank is obvious.

As to the possibility of budgeting the interest subsidy in advance for several years, such a practice is possible in some countries. In others, where budgetary commitments must be confined to one year, allocations during the first period of subsidization, when allocations of the IBRD and IMF would be sufficient, could be accumulated and used in subsequent years. Of course, the usual government allocations to IDA, even at a minimal level, could be used for that purpose and would be much more effective as an interest subsidy through the multiplier effect than otherwise.

Thus, the Horowitz Proposal can be summarized as an attempt to build a bridge between capital markets and the underdeveloped nations and to make it possible to borrow hard and lend soft and to assure a high priority for the flow of resources to underdeveloped nations. The proposal is not a panacea and could not, by itself, solve the problem of capital supply to the underdeveloped world; it could, however, be one of several promising channels for the provisions of development capital.

In the first place, it has a multiplier effect: by relatively small amounts and a system of guarantees, it sets free very substantial capital sums. It would work like an ignition spark, liberating energy far beyond itself.

Second, it provides for concessionary terms. The stipulations of loans to developing countries are not less important than the size of them. The snowballing process of repayment could nullify the benefits of any flow of capital. The cumulative dynamite of repayment is what we have called the time bomb in that flow. That is why provisions of funds for the IDA should have priority over all other agencies of aid.

Third, it permits a multilateral flow of capital and prevents political strings being attached to economic aid.

Fourth, it provides for access to capital markets. These are expanding and will expand even more with the growth of the GNP of the developed countries and progressively with the perfection of their mechanisms, in particular in Europe. If a multilateral institution serves as an instrument to secure ready access by the developing nations to the markets, it will make for a constant flow of capital, independent of political and temporary decisions.

Fifth, it is flexible and represents a middle path between direct private enterprise, which has failed so far to ensure the necessary flow of capital, and the tedious and difficult method of direct budgetary allocations.

Sixth, interest payments are drawn each year from an increasing GNP and, in most countries, from rapidly increasing budgets, and thus the burden is relatively declining.

Seventh, interest is paid to the citizens of the developed

country that lends the money to the underdeveloped country, and thus the transfer of resources from the borrowing (underdeveloped) to the lending (developed) country on account of interest is precluded for a number of years.

Eighth, the obligation of the treasury of the developed country arising from this interest subsidy is reduced by the taxation of income from bonds.

There are, to be sure, certain hindrances in some developed countries to implementation of the proposal, as reflected in the following observations in the survey by UNCTAD's Secretariat for the Third Committee: *Issues and Proposals:* "One of the principal difficulties hitherto encountered in obtaining support for this (the Horowitz) scheme lies in the fact that some of the most highly developed capital markets are to be found in countries currently under the heaviest balance-of-payments pressure." However, this difficulty could be met by such an allocation of loans raised within the scope of the proposal as would make certain that the total of the loans authorized for and spent by recipient countries was composed of the relevant currencies approximately in accordance with their balance-of-payments position.

That fund could be fed by government grants, the surplus profits of the World Bank, and allocations from funds created by the IMF through the medium of the special drawing rights. If these sources are taken into account, together with the fact that the total sum is quite modest—$50 million to $60 million per annum for each billion dollars of transfer of capital to be raised by the whole developed world—and that the interest payment would not encumber the balance of payments at all, seeing that the interest subsidy would be paid to bond holders who are citizens of the country providing it, there should be little trouble in implementing the plan.

As to the security offered for the bonds sold in the market, whose equivalent would be lent to IDA, there is a wide range of possible ways of providing collateral; some of them are fully set out in a report by UNCTAD's Secretariat. The capital of the World Bank alone suffices to provide such a guarantee, but, as said, it could be supplemented by additional guarantees from developed countries, as suggested in the report by UNCTAD's Secretariat.

The most specious of the arguments advanced against carrying out the Horowitz Proposal and of other measures to swell the flow of capital to underdeveloped countries is that of the tight money market. The market will always be tight, as long as the curve of economic activity is rising; only conditions of recession will loosen it. The EEC report just cited bears repetition in this context: "the present shortcomings of the capital markets are due not so much to insufficient savings as to the impossibility of adjusting correctly supply and demand on markets that are too narrow."

A stagnant economy, with a reduced demand for capital, would realign the supply of funds and the demand for them on the capital markets on a lower level. Is that really desirable? The palpable correlation of accelerated economic growth and tightness of capital markets, caused by added demand for capital, results in the paradox that ostensibly the greater the prosperity and the larger the increment of the GNP of the developed world, the more restricted are the chances of augmenting the capital flow to the developing world because prosperity, full employment, and rapid economic growth go hand in hand with tight money markets.

The answer, naturally, is to be found in the order of priorities. One can, as well, always make markets tight by economic policy that enlarges effective internal demand and investment among highly developed peoples. These manifestations are, in marked degree, a function of policy and can be escalated at will.

The report by UNCTAD's Secretariat shows that capital markets expand, especially in Europe, even for international issues, but all this extra money is funneled to developed economies that are already overheated and where more investment generates inflationary pressures. This economic supercharging and the danger or actuality of inflation tend to tighten capital markets and raise interest rates. Unprecedented welfare, galloping activity, and shortage of funds are, as it were, a troika. The upshot is a reluctance to extend economic aid. Disappointment with the products of economic development so far achieved by developing countries and the spirit of economic isolationism that has the West in its grip reinforce that hesitancy. Stresses and strains in manpower and capacity of production and inflationary pressures are evident everywhere. They do not make diversion of assets to economic aid any easier. Capital markets become unduly strained.

To acquiesce in this psychological attitude and surrender to the prevalent economic mood may spell a freeze in the appallingly low standards of living of two-thirds of the human race, with all the political perils to universal peace and stability with which that consequence is fraught. The affluent sector of the world cannot insulate itself from the repercussions of these ominous rumblings or remain a quiet island in the midst of a stormy ocean, an oasis of prosperity in a desert of desperate impoverishment.

In every area of economic endeavor, investment in the widest sense is the "open sesame" of progress and expansion, and the most vivid example is in agriculture. To expand it and to enhance the supply of food are the most urgent concerns of the underdeveloped world. Yet, with the measure of land that can still be brought under cultivation constantly diminishing, any such improvement depends overwhelmingly on larger yields per unit, and that can be realized only by irrigation, soil betterment, a sufficiency of fertilizers, and the like—all dependent on input of capital. The development of manufactures in countries that as yet have no industries to

available. Never could $2,609 million have been got together by budgetary votes, over and above present commitments of donor states. It is of paramount necessity to expand this access to international markets for funds that could then be advanced on concessionary terms, and all the more so in view of the difficulty in securing the budgetary provision, which had been the only source of funds for the IDA hitherto.

The hard truth is that, while in the period 1950–1960 credits and grants from all sources went up at an average annual rate of 15 per cent, the nominal growth since 1961 has been zero.

This alarming deceleration of aid to developing countries, taken together with their overpriming, in many instances, in respect to conventional loans, would ultimately mean a perpetuation and even a widening of the present gulf between the developed and underdeveloped worlds.

Members of the highly authoritative group of experts appointed by UNCTAD define the situation thus:

> Still more serious is the prospect that, if present trends continue, per capita incomes in the majority of the less-developed countries will show little or no increase, and the disparities in standards of living between the rich and the poor nations of the world will be greater at the end of this decade than at the beginning.[15]

The establishment of the World Bank and of the International Monetary Fund at Bretton Woods was a seismic departure. It set on foot measures for the access of developing nations to capital markets. What is needed now is to take one step further on the way to the transfer of resources from the developed and industrialized to the developing world.

If complications of transfer of payments on an excessive scale are to be avoided, the conditions of credit to developing countries must be formulated on capacity to pay. This prin-

15 *International Monetary Issues and the Developing Countries,* TD/B/32; TD/B.C.36.

ciple, so lucidly expounded by Keynes in *The Economic Consequences of the Peace,* in the ambit of reparations from Germany after the Treaty of Versailles, ought to be applied now if we are to learn the useful lesson of the past.

In appraising the scope of the capital market, one argument used to prove the difficulty of applying the principle is the absence of any a priori identity between countries with developed capital markets and those with surpluses in the balance of payments. This is true. It should, however, be borne in mind that the government of the United States does not consider the balance-of-payments limitation pertinent to funds raised for underdeveloped countries on its capital markets. The evidence is that the issues of such countries are exempted from the interest equalization tax, a concession naturally conceived as a stimulant and incentive to use of the U.S. capital market for the purpose.

TABLE 3-1

Value of New Foreign Bond Issues (in Millions of U.S. Dollars)
Purchased by U.S. Residents, 1952–65

Year	Foreign government issues	All issues
1952	268	295
1953	266	287
1954	284	316
1955	132	138
1956	386	467
1957	527	625
1958	811	912
1959	574	654
1960	455	550
1961	236	496
1962	656	1,016
1963	689	1,214
1964	795	1,080
1965*		1,340

* Preliminary estimate based on a 24 per cent increase in the amount of new foreign bonds offered in the United States from 1964 to 1965. Estimate for foreign Government issues in 1965 is not available.

Source: U.S. Department of Commerce.

Moreover, in both the United States and Europe, assessment of the potentialities of the capital market cannot be static; it should take into account the considerable dynamic development and expansion of the markets. It is the potentialities that matter, and, judged by past experience, they are very substantial.

Table 3-1 indicates the extent of the U.S. market for foreign issues. To what extent did the underdeveloped countries avail themselves of the opportunities of this market, not least considering the tax concession allowed? Table 3-2 supplies an answer. Only 18.5 per cent of the whole capital market outflow through this channel was absorbed by developing countries (Latin America, 10.5 per cent; other areas, 8 per cent). This, of course, is the direct result of a dearth of sufficient collateral in these countries. If the World Bank or IDA would agree to act as intermediary, the absorption could be greatly enlarged.

TABLE 3-2
Source of New Foreign Bond Issues Purchased by U.S. Residents,
1962–64

Source	Value millions of U.S. dollars	Per cent of all issues
Europe	454	13.7
Canada	1,870	56.5
Latin America	349	10.6
Japan	203	6.1
International institutions	89	2.7
Australia, New Zealand, South Africa	81	2.4
Other areas	265	8.0
TOTAL	3,311	100.0

Source: U.S. Department of Commerce.

A similar picture is presented by the German market, where the rise is even more spectacular; this is indicated in Table 3-3. Underdeveloped countries have a negligible share in the German market (see Table 3-4).

TABLE 3-3
Net Value of Purchases of Foreign Bonds by German Investors, 1957–65

Year	Value (million D.M.)
1957	21.0
1958	92.0
1959	344.6
1960	44.8
1961	12.0
1962	96.5
1963	107.1
1964	890.3
1965	1,357.9

Source: Monthly report of the Deutsche Bundesbank (February, 1966).

As to the total capital market of Europe, *The Swiss Economy in 1965,* a survey published by the Swiss Credit Bank, says, "Overall, international bond issues for their account and that of other borrowers mobilized $1.3 billion in Europe in 1965, compared to $800 million in 1964 and only $400 million in 1963."

TABLE 3-4
Source of Foreign Bonds Publicly Issued in Germany, 1963–65

Source	Value (millions of U.S. dollars)	Per cent of all issues
United States, Europe	441.3	76.2
Japan	125.0	21.6
Others	12.5	2.2
TOTAL	578.8	100.0

Source: Deutsche Bundesbank.

In all these large figures, what stands out is that, for all practical purposes, two-thirds of humanity is excluded from the capital markets of the developed world simply because of a lack of security to offer. Not only are these people denied any priority in those markets, but they cannot penetrate them at all, in spite of their rapid expansion. By force of circumstances, the markets are monopolized by the developed countries, with the overheated economic activity, the shortage of labor, the high standards of living, and the astonishing rate of growth.

Within the *mise en scène* of world development, it is unquestionably desirable and feasible that the developing countries should be placed in a position to absorb at least a part of the increment of foreign issues, and it is, therefore, crucial that a bridge be built between them and these capital markets. Interest limitations can be surmounted by the Interest Equalization Fund, and, even if a higher price is paid for the money, the difference, to be covered by the Fund, will stay within reasonable bounds. Bolder plans than this have materialized, and the reason aid and flow of capital are stagnating is to be sought in the realm of the spirit and not of material limitations.

At least an attempt should be made to try another way out—one, in effect, less revolutionary and unorthodox than the previous experience of the establishment of the World Bank in 1945 or the Marshall Plan in 1947–48, both of which were trail-blazing departures in the mode and magnitude of voluntary transfer of resources from the rich lands to the poor on an international scale. These novel uses of public funds to foster and further the economic growth of peoples had no historical precedent; they represented a radical turn of events in world history.

Against this experience, Pierre-Paul Schweitzer, the managing director of the International Monetary Fund, in an address before the U.N. Economic and Social Council on February 24, 1966, described what is happening today:

> Acute poverty has persisted in many countries, along with hunger and even the fear of famine. The gap between rich and poor countries remains painfully wide, with the advance of the poorer countries proceeding too slowly, and often suffering grievous setbacks.

At the same time, there has been an unrivaled growth of world trade, a sustained and high level of economic activity in much of the world, and a solid strengthening of international monetary cooperation. . . . We are all acutely aware that hundreds of millions of the world's people still live under deplorable conditions. . . .

We should, at the same time, recognize that an adequate solution of the problems of the developing countries will not flow automatically from the growing affluence of a relatively few rich nations. This will require a sustained effort by all countries, over many decades.

The poor nations cannot save and cannot invest. They will become poorer and poorer if new measures and ways to finance development are not explored and tested.

There is an opportunity to provide new facilities for financing the development of underdeveloped countries by the international community's creating additional liquidity in the world economy. A resolution adopted by the IMF conference in Rio de Janeiro in 1967 to make new special drawing rights available would, if implemented, signal the creation of new purchasing power by the international community to augment a liquidity that is not sufficient to maintain full and rapid economic growth and to finance an international trade that is growing at an annual rate of 8 per cent. The fact that in the last two years national reserves did not expand and that the whole of the newly mined gold was taken up for industrial and ornamental purposes and for hoarding made the innovation necessary and, indeed, urgent, if a deflationary contraction of world trade was to be prevented. What is intended is an annual injection of some $3 billion of new liquidity into the world economy. Considering that the total global product of developed and underdeveloped countries taken together comes to over $2,300 billion, this is a tiny extra, which could not have any serious inflationary impact.

Whether this supplementary liquidity might not serve a

dual purpose—helping to finance international trade and stimulating economic growth in the underdeveloped world—was discussed. It is frequently asserted that there should be no nexus between the creation of reserves and the provision of capital for the developing countries. This is getting to be another shibboleth founded on rigid prejudice, with little justification in the realities of the situation. It is possible, though it would be difficult, to insist that no special reserves should be created for the specific purpose of development; even this is a doubtful proposition. But it is less easy to understand why, if reserves are created by a consensus that there is need for more international liquidity, a modest portion of them could not be used for development. Is it fear of universal inflation, if a few hundred million dollars a year are set aside in a world in which the global GNP aggregates some $2,300 billion and the anticipated annual growth rate in reserves, thanks to special drawing rights, should be about $3 billion? The dogma of complete separation of development from creation of new liquidity cannot be rationally explained. A group of experts on the highest possible level, appointed by UNCTAD in 1965, rejected it and strongly recommended that part of the liquidity be allocated for development, with a view to swelling the flow of developmental finance to developing countries. There should be a firm bond between liquidity creation and development. There is no rational or reasonable argument, but only bias, against using newly created reserves of liquidity in part for development.

The purchase of IDA bonds by the IMF with monies arising out of newly created liquidity would have an invigorating effect first of all on the capital goods industry, as IDA would use its funds to underwrite projects of development, which engender a demand for new equipment. On the other hand, if approval of tariff preferences for the developing countries is expressed in practical measures, as envisaged by the UNCTAD resolution in New Delhi, namely:

. . . that the objectives of the generalized nonreciprocal, non-discriminatory system of preferences in favour of the developing countries, including special measures in favour of the least advanced among the developing countries, should be:

    a. to increase their export earnings
    b. to promote their industrialization
    c. to accelerate their rates of economic growth

then the resultant larger flow of consumer goods from the developing countries could enter the markets of the developed world and partly pay for the new equipment.

A remark of the U.N. Secretary-General, U Thant, in February, 1968, is pertinent: "The developed countries find themselves short of labor and even of capital, and yet they are protecting the inefficient use of both these resources in sectors of agriculture and industry which could be much more efficiently supplied from developing countries." This protectionism would be understandable if there were large-scale chronic unemployment in the developed countries, but this is "very far from the situation that prevails," the Secretary-General added.

Utilization of the great potential of idle manpower in underdeveloped countries to supply consumer goods to the developed ones is, therefore, a precondition of the global bloodless economic revolution that would so immensely amplify the resources, production, and living standards of the world at large. It would involve a swifter concentration of the developed economies on production of capital goods and the freer access to its extensive markets of consumer goods produced in the underdeveloped economies.

A blend of the Horowitz Proposal with the use of new liquidity reserves for development, for access by developing countries to capital markets and, for good measure, at least a maintenance of the present grants-in-aid, could revolutionize the present state of things.

National wealth cannot be expanded magically and speedily in the highly developed countries, where full employment is already the rule and further increment of the GNP depends on further technological advances. But, in the developing countries, there is a gigantic reserve of unemployed and underemployed manpower, with low productivity, and an excessive proportion of agricultural labor yielding a relatively low output. Added capacity there, brought about by adequate import of capital, would make new forces available and mean an economic revolution, with the wealth thus produced seeping into every part of the world's population and, besides, enriching the nations of high development even more.

Such a vision requires a statesmanlike approach, transcending the narrow horizons of a bookkeeper. It could be economically sound. And the choices are unmistakable: on the one hand, famine, political instability, perhaps war; on the other, eradication of poverty and unprecedented affluence and prosperity for all mankind.

What is needed is imagination and a political will to respond to the challenge. What is needed is the spirit that fired civilization after the Second World War, the spirit of the Bretton Woods Conference, a spirit the affluence has dimmed.

The Keynesian revolution did more to change the economic conditions of the developed world than any sanguinary clash of agonizing conflict. The integration between the developed and the developing world is a pioneering task and calls for a sense of history if the perilous abyss between promise and performance is to be safely crossed.

4 *The Strategy of the War Against Poverty*

The abolition of poverty belongs to the sphere of normative economics as an objective of economic policy. The two targets of this policy are to bridge the gap between the developed and the underdeveloped parts of the world and to eliminate marginal but by no means negligible pockets of poverty amidst underprivileged minorities within the developed world.

The first target was defined by the United Nations:

> It is an extraordinary fact that at a time when affluence is beginning to be the condition, or at least the potential condition, of whole countries and regions rather than of a few favoured individuals, and when scientific feats are becoming possible which beggar mankind's wildest dreams of the past, more people in the world are suffering from hunger and want than ever before. Such a situation is so intolerable and so contrary to the best interests of all nations that it should arouse determination on the part of advanced and developing countries alike, to bring it to an end.[1]

To achieve this target is made particularly difficult by the population explosion, reflected in projections of world popu-

[1] U.N. Department of Economic and Social Affairs, *The United Nations Development Decade, Proposals for Action,* Report of the Secretary-General, Doc. E/3613 (New York, 1962), p. v.

lation against the background of its growth in the past (see Table 4-1). Such projections foreshadow a rise in the population of the world from some 3.4 billion in 1967 to about 7.5 billion in another generation.

TABLE 4-1
Summary of U.N. World Population Projection (in Billions), 1960–2000

		Constant fertility		High variant		Medium variant		Low variant	
	1960	*1980*	*2000*	*1980*	*2000*	*1980*	*2000*	*1980*	*2000*
World	3.0	4.5	7.5	4.6	7.0	4.3	6.1	4.1	5.5
Developed regions	1.0	1.2	1.6	1.2	1.6	1.2	1.4	1.2	1.3
Developing regions	2.0	3.3	5.4	3.3	5.4	3.1	4.7	3.0	4.2

Source. Goran Ohlin, *Population Control and Economic Development* (Paris: Development Center of the Organization of Economic Cooperation and Development, 1967), p. 21.

Even more alarming is the shift in population distribution from the developed to the underdeveloped countries, so that, with this substantial supplement of numbers, the share of the underdeveloped countries in the world population would rise from two-thirds to four-fifths.

Progress toward a higher average level of living in the world as a whole is held back also by the shifting balance of population distribution which results from higher rates of population growth in developing countries than in wealthier countries. As the developing countries account for a larger and larger proportion of world population increases, they tend to offset the improvement of conditions in the world as a whole, which would otherwise be brought about by the gains in individual countries. At any rate, the actual number of human beings living in distress and unacceptable poverty has almost certainly increased rather than diminished. This is the combined result of the rapid growth of population in the poorer countries and their failure to join fully in the general march of progress. Even in education, a field in which many underdeveloped countries have made important achievements during the last decade, the progress has not been enough to justify any complacency. In spite of the efforts to stamp out illiteracy, the number of illiterate people may increase rather than diminish, as a result of the relentless growth of population.[2]

The maldistribution of income between the two parts of the world is as follows: of a total world population of 3,220 million in 1964, 1,011 million (31.4 per cent) were in the developed countries, with a total income of $1,372 billion (87.4 per cent), while 2,209 million people in the developing countries (68.6 per cent) had only 12.6 per cent of the world's income, $198 billion. Income per capita in 1964 was $1,357 in the developed countries, as compared with only $98 in the developing countries. This disparity of income, in steadily deteriorating circumstances, must exert greater pressure on resources.

However, economic analysis inclines more and more to discard the rigid formulas for the definition of overpopulation based on mere "arithmetical density" and on a ratio of population to natural resources. The idea of an optimum population holding good for all time is also dismissed, and it is being recognized that, even if the optimum is exceeded, it may be reestablished by capital accumulation and technical progress.[3]

Given such conditions, the transfer of mobile resources, the import of capital and skill, and the investment and effec-

[2] *Ibid.*, p. 7. For the purpose of this comparison, the census figures have been adjusted to take account of differences in geographical coverage of the 1951 and 1961 enumerations. The uncorrected figures show an even larger increase in the number of illiterates.

[3] D. V. Glass, *Population—Policies and Movements in Europe* (London: Oxford University Press, 1940), pp. 369–70: "But there is no optimum that holds good for all time, and the community may in any case decide to forego part of an increase in national income in order to retain a greater physical spaciousness of life. On the other hand, even if population were above the optimum at the time, the community might decide to maintain that population because of the difficulties which might be met during the transition period while numbers were falling to the theoretically desirable level, and because, owing to capital accumulation and technical progress, the old excessive size might soon become the new optimal size."

tive demand generated by them could apply momentum to economic development and growth. But, for the time being, because of a yawning investment gap between the developed and the underdeveloped countries, the dynamics of economic growth are bound to disimprove the present situation.

On the other hand, the growth of population in the underdeveloped parts of the world opens up new economic possibilities, if the vast propensity to consume could be transformed into effective demand. The expansion of purchasing power in these multitudinous agglomerations of humanity would, through marketing facilities, impart a stimulus to production, and the immense potential of underutilized manpower would contribute to the wealth and resources of the whole world and add significantly to the production of material goods on a global scale.

The underdeveloped countries, with incomes well below what is considered the poverty line in the developed countries, concentrate on the production of primary products. They are afflicted by hunger, disease, and ignorance, and the investment disparity between them and the developed countries presages an even wider economic gap. Low productivity and low income, redundant labor, unemployment and underemployment, and a shortfall in food supply are the symptoms of these afflictions. The lack of mobile resources such as capital and skill, in plentiful supply in the developed parts of the world, is responsible for the very limited share of secondary and tertiary stages in the total production of the underdeveloped parts.

Private capital is not attracted to countries of low productivity, short of skilled labor and scientific institutions and with restricted markets. Government and other international aid is relatively on the decline and in retrogression, owing to political and mental reservations and to difficulties in the balance of payments in the developed countries. The debt explosion clogs the channels even more, and the flow of capital is cut by large repayments on account of principal and interest. In the circumstances, the general and, even more so, the per head growth of the GNP is slowed up. Thus, in the underdeveloped countries there is a concentration of poverty and, withal, of a potential of production, and the tremendous gap in productivity between the developed and underdeveloped parts of the world betokens incalculable possibilities for development.

In the developed world, the rate of demographic growth is less than half of that in the underdeveloped world. The occupational distribution reflects an overwhelming proportion of the population in the high-income secondary and tertiary stages of production, with all trends and tendencies marking that further shift to occupations determined by the pattern of consumption, which is a concomitant of high incomes.

As to the future, the occupational changeover from primary and secondary to tertiary stages of production in highly developed, industrialized societies may to some extent retard the rate of growth of their GNP, as there is only a limited range of opportunities to step up productivity in services. The trend is counterbalanced in part by technological progress, but it is doubtful whether it could be offset entirely. Further, the preference for leisure and shortening of working time may also be reflected in some slowing down of the growth of the GNP in developed countries.

Even if the present rate of per capita rise in overall economic growth is sustained in spite of these inhibiting factors, the shift from production of goods to production of services would decelerate the rise in the total quantity of material goods available on a global scale, unless the underemployed labor reserve in the underdeveloped countries is drawn into the orbit of production of goods. Therefore the utilization of this reserve and equipment of its surplus manpower with capital goods are imperative for enhancing welfare and raising living standards globally.

In the developed states, the virtual extinction of the gap between underutilized capacity of production and actual production and full employment and the redistributive system of the welfare state hasten the trend toward more equality and narrow the distance between social classes, so that only small marginal pockets of frictional unemployment are left in the underprivileged sections of their populations. In the developed parts of the world, standards of living are rising sensationally, and the gap between classes is narrowing, while the poverty-stricken, underprivileged sections are a much smaller percentage of the population. Yet a growing sensitivity to social pressures makes even this residual destitution a source of political, racial, and social tension.

Overliquidity, overinvestment, and overemployment often exert inflationary pressures. The overheated economy with high productivity crashes against the barrier of limited manpower, and with labor on a seller's market its problems are accentuated, whereas the diffusion of wealth, the spread of social security, and the built-in stabilizers of the economy fortify the factors making for steadiness.

Further expansion is circumscribed by the fact that, to prevent inflationary pressures, some underutilization of plant and manpower is indispensable. The introduction of an incomes policy on a national scale did not eliminate the danger of inflation in a fully employed economy. The incomes policy could not be vindicated against formidable economic and social pressures.

The warring trends in the developed and underdeveloped parts of the world cannot be brought into equipoise by redistribution of manpower. The abatement of migratory phenomena today is the direct outcome of political, racial, and cultural considerations and objections to shifts of population, reinforced by trade union hostility and the resistance of other groups. The opposition to Asian entry into Britain and the maintenance of rigid quotas in the United States are cases in point. No mass migration from the underdeveloped to the developed countries can be expected in these circumstances, and the problem of redistribution of resources accordingly assumes particular significance. The need for that redistribution coincides with the shift in weight and importance from natural to mobile resources and the substitution of mobile for natural resources.

Irrespective, however, of natural resources, if skill and capital—namely, mobile resources—are augmented, the result is high productivity and high incomes and a shift to secondary and tertiary stages of production. The assumptions that "economic progress clearly can be made by increasing production per head in the sphere of primary, secondary and tertiary industry or by transferring labour from less to more productive spheres" and that "generally speaking, the main dynamic of economic advances has been rising income per head in either secondary or tertiary industry, often in both, and the transfer of population away from primary industry" are verified by experience all over the world.[4]

With a larger proportion of the population engaged in the secondary and tertiary stages of production, income per head and standards of living rise in parallel, and the tendency toward redistribution of resources, not of people, is strengthened, and the change in the composition of resources necessary for economic growth in a modern technological society lends it further backing.

The transition from primary to secondary and tertiary stages of production in the developed countries, the expansion of markets for manufactured products, the rising standards of living and consumption patterns that favor the use of manufactured products and services, the high component of capital in modern production, cheap transport for foodstuffs,

[4] Colin Clark, *The Conditions of Economic Progress* (London: Macmillan, 1940), pp. 11, 12.

raw materials, and fuel, the growing importance of synthetic materials—all this conduces to freedom from dependence on local resources and builds up the relative weight of mobile transferable resources such as capital and skill. Witness the breath-taking expansion of manufacturing industries in countries with no, or few, raw materials of their own, such as Hong Kong and Israel.

It is not paucity of natural resources that holds back the economic growth of underdeveloped countries. Most of them have abundant supplies, and, wherever natural resources are meager, substitution of mobile resources from other countries could be the answer, given the presently hard-to-come-by capital and skill. Private capital has little if any incentive to flow to underdeveloped countries, except for the exploitation of oil. Economic aid at the present level is inadequate. The investment gap may entail perpetuation of the existing divergence in standards of living and in the rate of growth of the GNP per capita. The distance between the developed and underdeveloped parts of the world would grow. The importance of transfer of capital, even preferable to its formation, is stressed by the need to expand purchasing power and consequently consumption and marketing facilities in the underdeveloped countries as one of the major impulses and stimuli of economic growth.

Unexploited resources of labor are available in the underdeveloped countries, while, in the developed ones, shortage of labor and inflationary pressures seem to establish the necessity for a rearrangement in the pattern of production and for export of capital to underdeveloped countries to encourage a more rational distribution of resources.

The inescapable conclusion, then, is that the strategy of development of the underdeveloped world must apply itself sedulously to the issue of demography. It is true that valiant efforts are made by certain governments, particularly that of

India, to arrest and control the rise of population, and it is theoretically possible to do so. Only in Japan, however, has there been success. The psychological, cultural, and religious impediments to family planning are tremendous, and few states can claim notable progress along the path of more rational demographic growth. But effort must continue, for without demographic strategy the widening gap in standards of living between the developed and underdeveloped worlds will never be bridged; rather, it will become wider and deeper. The rise in the GNP per head in the underdeveloped countries is seen to be insignificant, although economic growth in most of them has been slightly swifter than in the developed world. Natural increase, however, neutralizes that advantage to a great extent, and, at their present pace of demographic and economic progress, the doubling of a national annual income of $100 per head per annum would take several generations.

If further proof is demanded of the case for focusing attention on the population explosion as the crucial problem and perhaps the main limiting factor of economic progress, the following may serve:

> The simple and incontestable case against rapid population growth in poor countries is that it absorbs very large amounts of resources which may otherwise be used for increased consumption and, above all, for development. . . . The stress and strain caused by rapid demographic growth in the developing world is actually so tangible that there are few planners and economists of these countries who doubt that per capita incomes would be increased faster if fertility and growth rates were lower—indeed, in some cases they might otherwise not increase at all.[5]

But there is also a different, positive aspect to the economy

[5] Goran Ohlin, *Population Control and Economic Development* (Paris: Development Center of the Organization of Economic Cooperation and Development, 1967), p. 53.

of a growing population, if only transfer of mobile resources corresponds to the rate of that growth. In the eighteenth and nineteenth centuries the mechanism of that kind of economy was the driving force behind the processes of economic advance. However, a rapid rise in population, unaccompanied by increment of material and other resources, such as skill, through internal formation or transfer of capital from maturer economies, is bound to mean a lowering of living standards or a contraction of investment, and the future will suffer in consequence.

All the same, under certain conditions, an economy of growing population may spur economic growth by creating effective demand, which sparks off expansion of production and investment and awakens dormant resources. A broad comparison of the growth of the industrial countries and that of the rest of the world from the time of the Industrial Revolution to the First World War obviously indicates a positive association between the two. Many economists have concurred with Hicks' view "that perhaps the whole Industrial Revolution of the last two hundred years has been nothing else but a vast secular boom, largely induced by the unparalleled rise in population."[6] Indeed, Hicks has conclusively proved that the Industrial Revolution was, to a very great extent, the function of an unparalleled rise in population.

The effect of rapid population growth is, above all else, a greater physical propensity to consume, and, as incomes are on or below subsistence level in the countries concerned, an even marginal rise in purchasing power will activate production and investment. In many cases, this expansion of the domestic market will provide the technical and economic minima for a number of industries.

[6] J. R. Hicks, *Value and Capital* (London: Oxford University Press, 1939), p. 302. See also Simon Kuznets, "Demographic Aspects of Modern Economic Growth," WPC/WP/389; and "Quantitative Aspects of the Economic Growth of Nations: I. Levels and Variability of Rates of Growth," *Economic Development and Cultural Change,* Vol. 1 (October, 1956), pp. 28–31.

Here is a salutary comment on the power of markets to attract economic enterprise:

> This connection is seen even more clearly if account is taken of the influence of the size of the population on demand, and through demand on production. Technical progress can be exploited for economic purposes only with the achievement of mass production, which is impossible without mass consumption. In this way, the size of the population has a great influence on the level of production of a country. It was thanks mainly to this influence that the increase in population from the 16th–18th century appeared to be such a blessing.[7]

Economies of scale are becoming more and more important in modern industry and, therefore, a growing population and an expanding domestic market may be of major significance in advancing economic growth. The following remarks are relevant:

> When numbers are growing rapidly there is a strong and fairly steady increase in the demand for almost every commodity, for food, for clothes, for housing, for coal, and for almost everything else that satisfies the multifarious wants of human life. To meet this increasing demand, the supply of the various commodities must be correspondingly increased. The labour required for this purpose is, of course, readily available, as a consequence of the growth of numbers. But goods are not produced by means of labour alone, but by labour in co-operation with capital equipment and with natural resources.
>
> Accordingly a condition of rapidly growing numbers gives rise to a need for a constant expansion of capital equipment and natural resources in almost every branch of production. Additional factories are required in the great majority of industries, additional land is required for the production of the foodstuffs and raw materials that are needed in increasing quantities; and additional means of communication and transportation are required to carry the additional goods to the

---

[7] Paul Mombert, *Grundriss der Sozialekonomik*, II Abteilung, "Wirtschaft und Bevoelkerung" (Tübingen: Verlag Mohr, 1914), pp. 68, 69.

consumers. In short, when numbers increase rapidly, there is need for a steady enlargement of productive capacity, in almost every part of the economic system.[8]

Of course, a rise in productive equipment and productive capacity must correspond to the rise in population. If its productive capacity is thus expanded, either by internal formation or by import of capital, an underdeveloped economy will be transformed from an agrarian to an industrial pattern, with a parallel swing from primary to secondary and tertiary stages of production and from a subsistence to an exchange economy. It goes without saying that the provision of new resources for an economy of growing population is not confined to capital but also calls for a substantial change in quality and technological level, but, to some extent, skill and technological adaptability are mobile and transferable, either by introducing foreign expertise or by providing training and education, and both, in turn, are dependent on the availability of capital.

In an economy of growing population, it is feasible to utilize existing resources more thoroughly; interchangeability of capital, space, and other resources is determinant and can yield results: "It is quite plausible that in very sparsely settled countries, a larger population would be better able to avail itself of its natural resources. There would be economies of scale, the division of labour would be facilitated by greater density of settlement, transportation costs would be smaller, and so forth."[9]

The repercussions of a growing population on agricultural production and industrial concentration alike will be favorable if the proportion of secondary and tertiary producers

[8] R. R. Kuczynski, T. H. Marshall, A. M. Carr Saunders, H. D. Henderson, Arnold Plant, *The Population Problem, The Experts and the Public* (London: Allen & Unwin, 1938), pp. 88–89.

[9] G. Ohlin, *Population Control,* p. 57.

rises.[10] Such transformation can be speeded, and it can assume the nature of an economic revolution if an entire economy is metamorphosed within a brief space of time; the population explosion then becomes a relative concept, almost wholly dependent on an abundance of resources, as, in developed nations with ample mobile resources, population growth may even promote economic development.

Husbandry is no longer the main pursuit of man: secondary and tertiary stages of production are preponderant. In modern industrial production, the share of labor and skill compared with the value of raw materials is rising. Synthetic materials are substituted for natural ones. The value of capital equipment per unit of production has increased, and the comparative share of the tertiary stage of production has risen. Because of these factors, effective demand gains in momentum, and provision of resources is eased by cheap and efficient transport and by the fact that mobile resources mean more than natural resources for economic growth. Given a sufficiency of resources of capital and skill, effective demand will help to launch and sustain the process of economic growth. In the developed parts of the world, fiscal, monetary, and income policy largely determines the level of that demand, and that has a far-reaching impact on the general level of economic activity. Economic policy, for example, was instrumental in curbing the cyclical fluctuations of industrialized countries by maintaining practically full employment and virtually closing the gap between potential capacity of production and actual output. In the postwar period, it was conspicuously successful, narrowing the scope of actual poverty in developed states to little more than a marginal manifestation.

[10] Institute of Pacific Relations, *The Peopling of Australia,* Series No. 4 (Melbourne: Melbourne University Press, 1933), p. 117: "The natural capacity of secondary industries to maintain and absorb population depends not only on the resources available, but upon the extent to which the home market has become large enough to provide opportunities for large scale production, and upon the use made of these opportunities. Natural growth is progressive and cumulative."

In the underdeveloped states, on the other hand, no measure of redistribution of incomes could impinge substantially on the widespread prevalence of abysmal poverty. Fiscal, monetary, and income policy could not of itself perform the function of raising average standards without a very sizeable transfer of resources from sophisticated economies. As the weight of these resources grew, they could not only furnish the capital required to expand productive capacity but, in some measure, could finance consumption. By adding to employment and, equally, by stimulating economic activity, they would raise effective demand in the domestic markets.

As far as concerns marketing facilities and maintenance of rising levels of consumption, the fairly large share of local financing—four-fifths of the total—in investment in underdeveloped nations is not altogether to the good. It implies diversion of resources from consumption in countries where consumption levels are already low and in a subsistence economy at that, whereas expanding investment, if financed by imported capital, public or private, has the consequence of maintaining consumption levels, at least of the workers engaged in establishing new or enlarging existing productive capacity.

While that expansion goes on, consumption by the labor-force that is employed in the investment sector is financed from external sources without diminution of the purchasing power of the population as a whole, and the corresponding output of goods is postponed, as a rule, until the new capacity of production comes into full operation. This effect is reinforced by expenditure on establishing the infrastructure indispensable for a new productive enterprise.

The effect of this two-pronged approach—a large investment sector in productive industry and the establishment of the infrastructure, both underwritten by external sources—will be twofold: improvement of the condition of the people through rising employment and, in the long run, higher efficiency of labor by virtue of better conditions; stimulation of

new output and the rendering of its absorption easier by enlargement of marketing facilities and a stepping-up of effective demand on the domestic market.

So it transpires how intimately linked, for an expanding
economy, are the extension of domestic markets and the creation of effective demand with the problem of providing capital, which will make directly for the establishment of new
productive capacity, but—indirectly, by financing consumption—make, also, for the extension of domestic markets.

Food supply is another aspect of the population explosion.
The problem of development and of the so-called Third
World is, indeed, mainly and predominantly one not of food
but of overall economic progress. Nevertheless,

> Large-scale hunger and undernutrition are not only spectres
> of the future but present realities in the poor countries, and
> it is obvious that their population growth will increase the
> demand for food considerably in the decades to come. . . .
> The most critical variable, once again, is time. It seems quite
> possible that in the course of the next century the world
> might settle down gently to a more or less stationary state. For
> the future, because population dynamics are sluggish and re-
> source developments a very long-time affair, it is essential to
> bear in mind always that the present rate of growth will in the
> course of some thirty to forty years require as much additional
> food as the entire present output merely to keep world popu-
> lation fed at present levels. In Latin America, where the rate
> of growth is particularly high, the additional amount of food
> necessary to stay put will be twice as large as present output.
> In order to raise the nutritional standards of the world to the
> accepted standards, additional supplies would have to be about
> 3.5 times as large as the current production of food in the
> world.[11]

The immediate and actual situation must be surveyed in
analyzing the ways and means of raising agricultural productivity, which is the catalyst of economic development in
underdeveloped countries, as a source, first, of food supply,

[11] G. Ohlin, *Population Control*, pp. 31, 32, 34.

second, of higher incomes, and, third, as a labor reserve for an occupational reshuffle in the economy as a whole. In the 1960's, food production in the underdeveloped world fell behind demand; the reasons are given in the study *The Food Problem of Developing Countries:*

> The 1960's has been called a "Decade of Development." It is therefore a matter for concern that in the first seven years of this decade the following phenomena have coincided:
> 1. food production in the developing countries, taken together, has grown more slowly than demand,
> 2. the area of good new land that could easily be brought under cultivation in developing countries has been sharply reduced,
> 3. the population of developing countries has been growing at an increasing rate,
> 4. the surplus stocks of grain in North America have roughly speaking been exhausted mainly through exports to less developed areas,
> 5. development aid from the richer countries has on the whole not increased, and
> 6. the debt burden of many developing countries has been rising fast.[12]

Food production per head diminished in the bulk of the underdeveloped world, as indicated in Table 4-2.

TABLE 4-2

Per Cent Change in Grain Crop Area, Yield, Output, and Per Capita Output in Major Regions, 1934–38 and 1960–66

	Crop area	Yield	Output	Per capita output
Latin America	33	8	42	— 16
Africa	29	20	54	8
Asia	32	7	41	— 2
Total less-developed	32	8	42	— 3

Source: Lester R. Brown, *Man, Land, and Food: Looking Ahead at World Food Needs,* Foreign Agricultural Economic Report No. 11, Economic Research Service, U.S. Department of Agriculture (November, 1963), tables 17, 18, 19, 21.

[12] OECD, *The Food Problem of Developing Countries* (Paris, 1968), p. 10.

Here is a combination of demographic, economic, and agro-technical factors that vex the problem of food supply. One is the repercussion of larger food imports on the balance-of-payments and the foreign exchange standing of underdeveloped countries.

Thus, although the recent agrarian revolution, a product of new departures in agricultural techniques and economic policy, may confidently be expected to continue:

> No conceivable increase in production will, however, suffice if the rapid population growth does not slow down very considerably in a not too distant future. No treatment of the food problem is therefore complete unless it contains a serious discussion of the questions raised by the present rates of population growth.[13]

According to the FAO, world food production rose from 1954 to 1964 by about 30 per cent and population by 22 per cent, so that the very low standards of nutrition, betrayed by the undernourishment and famine that torment about one-half of the world's population, could be improved only little. From the point of view of food supply, population growth is decisively important. If the objective is the abolition of poverty, the question

> . . . is not primarily whether world population grows very much larger than now, but whether its future growth will be compatible with reasonable economic conditions or a continued threat to economic improvement. There is some reason to think that spontaneous fertility decline will occur only when economic improvement is fairly rapid. If, on the other hand, continued high fertility nullifies the economic gains individuals reap from economic growth then the future growth of the world population will have built into it a vicious spiral of unchecked and rapid growth at levels of continued poverty.[14]

13 *Ibid.*
14 G. Ohlin, *Population Control*, p. 24.

As some 65 to 70 per cent of the two-thirds of humanity living in the Third World is engaged in primary, mainly agricultural, production, farm productivity is the mainspring of the strategy of war against poverty among them. A rise in that productivity means improvement in the supply of food, higher incomes, and, consequently, better standards of health, education, and efficiency. It would have a most favorable effect on the balance of payments and free labor to expand manufacturing industries and services, with rising standards of living as their reflection.

How much expansion of agricultural production signifies for the balance of payments is clear from the fact that only forty underdeveloped countries are not importers of food. The underdeveloped countries, between them, import over $4 billion worth of food each year, a stupendous outlay, which restricts their possibility of importing capital goods and therefore their development potential. The injurious effect on their economic growth needs no emphasis. If diversification of economies is a *sine qua non* of the progress and prosperity of the underdeveloped countries, then the raising of their agricultural productivity is the first step on the way to that diversification.

Transformation of agriculture in the underdeveloped countries is taking place in an environment where farm techniques and conditions are being rapidly and extensively revolutionized. Even this sector of the economy, which would seem to be more dependent on nature than any others, is heading toward emancipation from natural conditions. By its essence, it is tied to certain topographic, climatic, and other factors. It is rooted in the soil. But the ultimate limits set by nature are so elastic, so progressively open to expansion, that the full range of possibilities has never been exhausted. If agricultural production and a country's carrying capacity are seen as made up of soil, climate, capital, scope of markets, the skill of the farmers, and so forth, the impact of such natural elements as topography and climate may be regarded as lessening in comparison with the more artificial ones of capital, skill, technique, proximity of markets, and the rest. It may be said that the interchangeability of the natural and artificial elements is growing and that the process is fairly rapid, but the extent to which it becomes effective is determined not by technical and natural possibilities alone but by economic considerations. These trends in the elasticity of agriculture's natural limits may be summarized as follows:

> If we deal with the food supply question first, it is pertinent to state that theoretically the ultimate capacity of any country to produce food is set by its climate and topography. Over all other factors in agricultural production there is human control, which may be presumed ultimately to exploit natural conditions to the limit. However, in practice that stage is never reached, and the degree of productivity of any country at any time is a function of the economic factor, the climate factor, the soil factor and the "knowledge factor." The effect of the "soil factor" is closely correlated with the economic factor. For although, given the necessary climate, no soil is so poor that it cannot be made as productive as the richest natural soil, yet the degree of productivity attained at any moment is largely determined by the intensity of the system of agriculture followed, which in turn, is governed by economic circumstances.[15]

Expansion of agricultural production thus encounters two kinds of limitation: natural conditions, which, however, are more and more liable to the artificial influences of skill, capital, and so on and are very flexible; economic considerations in applying the expedients of skill and capital to transform and to deliberately shape natural conditions.

Rising productivity has partly liberated the volume of production from its tight dependence on area. C. H. Larsen, cal-

---

[15] C. B. Fawcett, "Some Factors in Population Density," *Problems of Population,* Report of the Proceedings of the Second General Assembly of the International Union for the Scientific Investigations of Population Problems, ed. G. H. L. F. Pitt-Rivers (London, 1932), p. 197.

culating the rise in harvests for the thirty years before the First World War, concluded that 20 per cent of it was due to a greater total area, 30 per cent to more intensive rotation, and 50 per cent to intensification.[16]

Interspatial and intertemporal comparisons go far to support the claim that the range between minimum and maximum yields per unit of land is so wide as to spoil any attempt to assess a country's technical and natural capacity to produce more and ever more foodstuffs. Table 4-3 gives interspatial

TABLE 4-3

Average Yields (100 Kilograms per Hectare) of Wheat, Maize, and Rice in Selected Countries, 1961–63

	Wheat	*Maize*	*Rice*
Tunisia	3.4	—	—
Jordan	5.2	—	—
Venezuela	5.3	11.0	15.3
Brazil	6.9	13.0	17.1
Pakistan	8.1	10.0	15.9
India	8.4	9.5	14.8
Iran	8.6	—	19.6
Colombia	9.1	11.2	19.5
Israel	10.0	40.4	9.7
Argentina	12.6	17.7	33.6
Chile	13.7	20.7	26.9
Sudan	16.0	8.2	—
Mexico	16.8	9.4	22.5
United States	16.9	37.8	39.5
Taiwan	19.7	17.5	32.1
United Arab Republic	25.1	24.0	52.3
Japan	26.1	25.9	50.5
Netherlands	43.8	38.4	—

Source: United Nations, Food and Agriculture Organization, *Production Yearbook, 1963* (New York, 1964).

comparisons for the period 1961–63. An intertemporal comparison (Table 4-4) demonstrates that the range of production within a given area is no less considerable. Considerable increases in crop areas occurred during the last two decades.

[16] Clark, p. 261.

TABLE 4-4

Per Cent Change in Area of Crops, Crop Output per Unit of Land, and
Crop Yields for Field Crops in Twenty-two Study Countries

Country	Time span	Annual rate of increase in crop output*	Area of crops	Field crop yield
Israel	1948–63	9.7	68.5	120.4
Sudan	1948–62	8.0	49.9	50.8
Mexico	1948–60	6.3	49.7	28.9
Philippines	1948–62	5.2	66.9	9.8
Tanganyika	1948–63	5.2	58.8	14.4
Yugoslavia	1948–63	5.1	6.8	33.2
Taiwan	1948–61	4.5	11.7	45.7
Turkey	1948–63	4.5	62.0	16.7
Venezuela	1953–62	4.5	54.0	14.1
Thailand	1948–62	4.4	29.5	23.8
Brazil	1948–62	4.2	54.6	5.9
Greece	1948–62	3.7	22.3	39.3
Iran	1948–63	3.6	38.6	12.5
India	1948–62	3.1	26.0	11.5
Poland	1948–63	3.0	− 0.9	30.4
Argentina	1948–63	2.8	2.7	18.6
Chile	1948–63	2.8	14.0	8.3
Japan	1948–63	2.8	0.9	24.7
Spain	1948–61	2.7	3.1	31.0
Colombia	1948–62	2.6	11.5	50.2
United Arab Republic	1948–63	2.0	6.2	20.1
Pakistan	1948–63	1.8	13.9	28.5

* Annual compound rates for field crops and other crops combined.

Source: U.S. Department of Agriculture, *Changes in Agriculture in 26 Developing Nations, 1948–63,* Foreign Agricultural Economic Report No. 27 (November, 1965).

Such rates of increase cannot be sustained indefinitely or even for very long, but during the critical decades ahead they will continue to be important.

In most of the cases reviewed, the extremes of low and high yields, more and less valuable crops, higher and lower productivity per farmer cannot be explained by natural conditions. Once more, the interchangeability of artificial and natural conditions seems to figure importantly.

What also makes for an extension of the bounds within

which the value of agricultural production may rise is the shift from less remunerative to more valuable crops. The tendency for this shift to be speeded up results from two distinct but dovetailed processes: the rise in national aggregate and per capita income of the more developed countries, and the progress of nutritional science, which tends to encourage the substitution of protective for energy-producing foods, or, rather, a change in the weights of these two ingredients of the national diet. This is explained by the possibility the rise in national aggregate and per capita income provides of buying the more expensive protective foods and the contributory change in taste, not to mention the exploits of modern nutritional science, with its emphasis on the virtue of protective foods, its denunciation of deficiencies in the consumption of them, and its vitamin discoveries.

It seems probable that in several countries the consumption of carbohydrates per head of the population has fallen, whereas the consumption of proteins has risen; changes have also taken place in the consumption of different kinds of animal and vegetable fats. Some indications of this probability are the lessening of the muscular labor required because of the extended use of machinery; the multiplication of that part of the population occupying itself chiefly with intellectual labor; and the general rise in food production.

The interplay of all those agents—high productivity of the soil per unit of land and per earner; the increased influence of knowledge and capital and the interchangeability of space, capital, and knowledge; the shift away from consumption of energy-producing to protective foodstuffs; the introduction of new cultures—has had far-reaching effects on agriculture, within an ambiance of innovations that include, as perhaps the most important, extensive use of fertilizers, expansion of irrigation, mechanization, cultivation of more paying crops, new crop varieties, and a better selection of seeds.

In all advanced countries, the weight of fruit, vegetables,

meat, and dairy produce in the average diet is rising; the share of cereals falling. This is partly because of a rising standard of living, which demands a more varied diet, partly because of the growing trend toward urbanization, which invariably results in a change of that kind, partly because of technological progress, which involves less strenuous physical labor and a consequent moving away from extensive consumption.

Self-sufficiency in foodstuffs is becoming rare. Concentration of population by area and fertility of soil is being broken up. Britain imports 77 per cent of its grain and flour, Germany 27 per cent; in Belgium, the Netherlands, Denmark, Sweden, and Switzerland, the import comes to 59 per cent.

Crop rotation, new methods of fertilizing and irrigating, and experimentation with new crops have combined to multiply the yield of each acre of land so much that old ideas about the size of a population a unit area can support must be radically revised. The upward graph of productivity is not at its end. As long as agricultural techniques continue to make such rapid progress, land area cannot be the yardstick for gauging absorptive capacity. In countries of new "colonization," the rise in productivity is even swifter, owing to the greater predisposition of settlers to adopt new methods.[17]

The range of possible rises in agricultural production is

[17] *The Peopling of Australia,* p. 198: "The importance of the 'knowledge' factor is seldom fully appreciated, yet Australia's development as a primary producer has depended largely upon it. The accumulated experience and skill of sheep breeders has been one of the greatest factors in her pastoral industry. The development of labour-saving machinery, on the one hand, and of special varieties of crop plants, on the other, have been of immense importance to the producers of cereals, especially wheat." Clark, p. 245: "The tremendous superiority of the new countries over the old is evident, and indeed the best results are shown in the most recently settled continent of Australia, followed by South America. Denmark leads Europe. . . . The greatest feats of productivity have been achieved in Australia and New Zealand where a people naturally skilled in breeding have been replanted on new and spacious soil."

widening in the postwar period. It is not confined to putting new areas under cultivation, but is concentrated mainly on raising yields:

> The possibilities of increasing yields are clearly in the long run very great indeed. Crop yields will be raised considerably by the introduction of new varieties, greater use of fertiliser and pesticides, and irrigation; these improvements are of course usually interdependent.
>
> The increased use of chemical fertiliser holds special promise even in the relatively short run. . . . It has been argued that with better varieties, pest control, and application of fertiliser on the Japanese scale, Indian rice yields could be raised to almost two and a half times their present levels.
>
> . . . Any inventory of the possible means to expand world agricultural output must conclude that we are very far indeed from seeing any abrupt and absolute barriers to such growth. It is evident that most of these improvements will require investments—in research, land improvement, storage facilities, agricultural machinery, etc.—and a considerable increase in nonagricultural inputs like fertiliser and pesticides.[18]

One of the most momentous reorientations in agricultural productivity has to do with new varieties. In Mexico new varieties of wheat doubled the yields per acre in the course of the 1950's. In Israel, agricultural research has helped to raise cereal yields from some 600 kilograms per hectare to over 5,000 on unirrigated lands, and from 3,000 to over 10,000 kilograms on irrigated land. To be sure, all this entails import of larger amounts of high-quality seeds, fertilizer, and pesticides, weighing heavily on the balance of payments:

> What is serious . . . is that for many years to come a number of developing countries are likely to face a difficult balance-of-payments situation. To develop, they must import large quantities of capital goods. If at the same time they have to import increasing amounts of food and serve a rising external debt, shortage of foreign exchange may force them to keep the econ-

---

[18] G. Ohlin, *Population Control,* pp. 33, 34.

omy growing slowly, so that neither production in general nor
the export capacity will expand in a way that will permit these
countries to obtain a sound, viable economic position in the
foreseeable future. It is here the real danger lies.[19]

Agricultural revolutions and rising productivity cannot be
divorced from the general development of the economy and
the society and from technological levels and educational
progress:

> . . . agriculture cannot develop in isolation. Its development
> depends on the expansion of a number of other activities. In
> fact, development of agriculture implies its gradual transfor-
> mation from a state of more or less pure subsistence agricul-
> ture to one of production for the market where it sells an in-
> creasing part of its produce to other sectors of the society and
> buys increasing quantities of productive inputs from them.
> . . . There will therefore always be a certain correlation be-
> tween development in agriculture and the more general de-
> velopment of society as a whole, not only of the agro-allied
> activities mentioned above.[20]

As more than half of the population of the world lives in
Asia, what is happening there matters decisively. In his
essay "The Agricultural Revolution in Asia,"[21] Lester R.
Brown asserts that "as of mid-1968, both the food situation
and food production prospects in Asia have changed almost
beyond belief." He mentions the self-sufficiency of the Philippines, the fact that Iran became a net exporter of wheat
that year, and that the rice harvest in Ceylon went up by 13
per cent. These tremendous advances he attributes in the
main to larger supplies of water and fertilizers and, even
more so, to the new high-yielding varieties of wheat, sorghum, and millet, showing that these often double the output of the traditional strains and thus accelerate and expand

[19] *The Food Problem of Developing Countries*, p. 108.
[20] *Ibid.*, p. 19.
[21] Lester R. Brown, "The Agricultural Revolution in Asia," *Foreign Affairs* (July, 1968), p. 689.

the process of agricultural development markedly. With enough water, two or even three crops per year are obtainable. Brown's conclusions are these:

> Problem areas notwithstanding, an agricultural revolution is under way in Asia. The new cereal varieties provide a means for tapping some of the vast, but as yet largely unrealized, food-producing potential of the tropics and subtropics, putting them on a more competitive footing with the temperate-zone cereal producers. The agricultural breakthrough occurring in several major Asian countries can be repeated in Latin America and Africa. Mexico, which once depended on imports for nearly half its wheat needs, is now exporting small quantities of both wheat and corn. Kenya, until recently a food-aid recipient, has produced an exportable surplus of corn, its food staple. Tunisia and Morocco are introducing the Mexican wheats. Much of the technology now being applied in Asia will also be applied in both Latin America and Africa, if the necessary top-level political and proper combination of economic policies are forth-coming.[22]

Japan is frequently cited as an example of rising agricultural productivity. Hiromitsu Kaneda records impressive testimony, the conclusion of which is that the rise in the interval in question must be about 40 per cent:

> On a per-farm basis, during the periods of 1952–54 and 1959–61 . . . in terms of annual rates of growth, the gain in planted area was 1.7 per cent per annum, in capital stock 2.2 per cent, in value added 3.3 per cent, and the decline in labor hours was 1.7 per cent per annum. This means that value-added per unit of labor in aggregate Japanese agriculture increased at 5.0 per cent per year during this period. Clearly, this is the period in which Japanese agriculture experienced the highest rate of growth in the productivity of labor.[23]

22 *Ibid.*, pp. 697–98.
23 Hiromitsu Kaneda, *The Sources and Rates of Productivity Gains in Japanese Agriculture, as Compared with the U.S. Experience* (New Haven, Conn.: Economic Growth Center, Yale University, 1967).

William S. Gaud, administrator of the U.S. Agency for International Development, describes the situation as follows:

> Record yields, harvests of unprecedented size and crops now in the ground demonstrate that throughout much of the developing world—and particularly in Asia—we are on the verge of an agricultural revolution. I call it the Green Revolution.
>
> New inputs and infrastructure, new attitudes, adequate farm credit, and sound policies are the active ingredients of this Green Revolution. And they are paying off. World agricultural production in 1967 set a new record, and the less-developed countries accounted for most of the increase. Total agricultural output in the developing nations rose by 7 to 8 per cent over 1966. Per capita food production increased by 6 per cent.
>
> This year, an estimated 16 million Asian acres are being planted to the improved varieties. Next year, the total could be 30 to 35 million acres or more.
>
> The world is on the brink of an unprecedented opportunity. The critical food problem of the next 20 years can be solved. A growing number of developing nations are now moving to solve it.[24]

The areas planted with these new varieties are expanding at a rapid pace; in Asia, they increased to 20 million acres in 1968.

The Green Revolution necessitates a huge investment of capital and much skill in controlling the new system of irrigation, the selection of seeds, and the extensive use of fertilizers. Thus the traditional agriculture is being rapidly subjected to far-reaching changes, and the process of transformation is bound to have its repercussions on the whole pattern of economy in the developing world.

A striking example of the possibilities inherent in the agricultural revolution is provided by Israel. A study made by the Economic Research Service of the U.S. Department of

[24] William S. Gaud, "The Green Revolution," *International Development Review* (June, 1968), p. 3.

Agriculture entitled *Changes in Agriculture in 26 Developing Nations, 1948–63* shows that Israel was first among nineteen countries in the value of agricultural output per farm worker, one of the two lowest in illiteracy, and the lowest in infant mortality. It analyzes the country's agricultural progress in these words: "Israel . . . has substantial increases in area of crops, in variable and fixed capital per hectare of arable land, in level of applied technology, and in the size of its agricultural labor force. It also ranked high in educational and health levels." Israel also led in annual rate of rise in crop output.

This process of modernizing agriculture and of augmenting the yield per unit of production began long before the establishment of the state of Israel. Lord Boyd-Orr, for instance, has this to say on the rise of farm productivity in Palestine before the Second World War:

> In the Jewish settlement in Palestine, agriculture has been raised to such a high level of efficiency that although the settlement only occupies 7 per cent of the total agricultural output, it is claimed that it produces about 50 per cent of the total agricultural output. To enable it to reach this high level of efficiency, however, there are three workers in other industries for one in agriculture.

During the period 1950–67, agricultural production rose by more than 450 per cent, and per capita production was tripled. The irrigated area was expanded fivefold. Herds of milch cows were tripled; the number of tractors was multiplied nine times. New crops and new methods of cultivation were introduced; notable advances were made in crop production and in the yield of livestock. Since the end of the Second World War, the export of citrus fruit has been tripled and the area of citriculture enlarged approximately threefold.

In the same period, the value of agricultural export rose

from $17 million to $109 million, and the share of domestic
production in the food supply from less than 50 per cent for
a population of about 1 million to more than 85 per cent for
one of 2.7 million, on an incomparably higher level of nutrition. The relatively fast improvement in productivity
went *pari passu* with a rapid expansion of productive capacity (see Table 4-5). Gross capital stock in agriculture rose

TABLE 4-5
Indicators of Expansion of Productive Capacity in Israel, 1952–67

	1952	1967	Per cent increase
Capital stock in agriculture (millions of 1967 dollars)	423.5	1,156.5	173
Gainfully employed (thousands)	85.0	105.9	25
Gross product (millions of 1967 dollars)	56.6	280.1	395
Value of capital stock per person employed	$5,000	$10,900	118.0
Value of gross product per person employed	$700	$2,600	271.0

Source: Research Department, Bank of Israel.

by 173 per cent, while the number of gainfully employed was
25 per cent higher in 1967 than in 1952. Employment rose
steadily until 1961: since then it has exhibited an almost
unbroken decline, and capital accumulation has slowed
down notably. The combined inputs of labor and capital
were practically constant in the period 1962–67, but their
stability was offset by higher productivity.

The chief factors of the changes in productivity were the
skills acquired by the newly settled farmers as they gained
experience in husbandry, a penetrating extension service of
professional instructors, and research. Typical examples are
shown in Table 4-6.

The improved productivity made it possible to maintain
the rise in income per employed, which was about 150 per
cent (calculated at constant consumer prices), between 1952
and 1967. Thus, an export-minded, highly mechanized, com-

TABLE 4-6
Per Cent Change in Average Yields per Unit of Land of
Selected Crops in Israel, 1955–65

Crop	Per cent change
Wheat	167
Barley	169
Oats	150
Maize for grain, irrigated	9
Sorghum for grain, irrigated	89
All field crops*	114
Cotton lint, irrigated	37
Milk	6
Eggs	18
Overall*	55

Source: Data compiled from *Statistical Abstract of Israel*, 1955–67.
* The figures shown are weighted averages.

puter-guided and planned husbandry displays a gamut of prospects for stepping up farm productivity, if one can count on the requisite inputs of capital and skill.

With modern technology, there is no doubt that rural production can be quickly, even spectacularly enlarged. Israel's experience in this respect is of particular interest, as the results were achieved by a population predominantly untutored in agriculture, which had to undergo an occupational reshuffle in an arid country with scarce natural resources including water. It was done mainly by the application of capital, know-how, and science. In a single decade, from 1955 to 1965, agricultural output went up by 156 per cent in real terms; employment on the land went up by 6.5 per cent only. The value of production per employed person rose by over 140 per cent, and its average is now ten times higher than in developing countries and higher than in France, Germany, or Japan. On 1 million acres, with only 12 per cent of the population engaged in farming, foodstuffs are produced for 85 per cent of the consumption of nearly 3 million, and, on top of that, farm produce to a value of $150 million is shipped or flows from the same tiny area to overseas markets. The worth of the total output by a relatively small number of farmers is over half a billion dollars. In some branches, such as milk production and cotton, Israel can claim the highest yield in the world per unit of production.

If the developing countries could expand their farm output by 1985 at the annual rate Israel attained—almost 8 per cent—the gap projected between the rising demand for foodstuffs and their supply could be closed and the standard of nutrition conspicuously improved. The specter of famine, perhaps the most terrifying feature of the population explosion, could be banished.

There is an inherent paradox in the situation: the explosion is detonated not by a rising birth rate but by lower mortality, particularly of infants, as a result of better hygiene and such medical devices as vaccination and prophylaxis and their wider availability. The boons of a falling death rate and sounder health are tragically indivisible from the danger of starvation because there is not enough food to sustain rapidly proliferating numbers. The condition is aggravated by maldistribution of population. The spurt of population is most pronounced in areas already short of food, in countries of low agricultural productivity, excessively dependent on food imports as it is, which is why the imbalance of food supply and population has been emphasized in recent decades. Despondency and despair about the possibility of breaking the vicious circle were amply warranted by the slow progress made toward solving this crucial problem. In some parts of the world, and certainly in Asia, per capita output was so static that large-scale imports of foodstuffs were necessary. However, recently the view of those who are persuaded that we have the knowledge, the resources, and the technology to redress the equilibrium between food and mouths has been vindicated.

Former U.S. Secretary of Agriculture Orville Freeman believes in the technological revolution in agriculture, whose "impact has been so great and its prospects so apparently limitless, that for the first time in history man can visualize a world without hunger.[25] In 1967, production of food rose by 3 per cent, average world population by 2.2 per cent. This would be only fractional progress. What is important is the distribution of the rise. It was mainly in the underdeveloped countries, with an average of 6 per cent, against a population rise of 3.6 per cent. A drop in food production was registered in Europe and the Soviet Union, where it would not entail starvation and would affect the standard of living only slightly.

For this, a technological breakthrough in agricultural production appears to be responsible and the principal factor in the rapid expansion in areas sown with new, high-yielding varieties of food grains. The potential harvest of the new varieties of wheat and rice is twice and three times the largest harvest of the strains in previous use. Splendid results were obtained in the production of rice. The Philippines, previously a net importer, became an exporter, and in some parts of India production has risen by as much as 30 per cent. Indeed, there are countries in Asia where it rose as much as fourfold, though in limited areas. This is a tremendous advance, but it does not yet ensure a solution of the food problem of the underdeveloped world, and the population explosion may still end in agricultural productivity being outrun by demographic growth.

The obstacles along the path to the spread of new methods of cultivation and of new varieties of food grains are many and menacing. In contradistinction to industry, it is not enough to master new ways and apply them widely through a technological elite of managers and engineers. The methods have to be conveyed to millions of humble peasants: the

---

25 Orville L. Freeman, *World Without Hunger* (New York: Praeger, 1968), p. 15.

traditional resistance of that class to innovation must be overcome and sociological and economic barriers torn down and
new economic conditions created. A general transformation
of agriculture in the underdeveloped world is sometimes as
formidably hedged in as are the incentives to achieve it.

Even the technological problems yet to be solved are complicated and difficult. The new varieties of food grains need
to be adapted to new conditions in a process of moderniza-
tion that involves more extensive use of chemical fertilizers,
better water control, new implements and machinery. The
supply of implements and fertilizers on so gigantic a scale
demands a superhuman effort. Prices, markets, capital supply, and other economic adjuncts are also of critical importance. Nevertheless, the breakthrough has been made; the
way to enhanced agricultural productivity is open.

At the same time, many millions now employed on the
land would be otherwise disposable. The multitudes thus
freed could be transferred to new production in other sectors
of the economy, first and foremost industry, and so add to
the overall wealth of nations. At the moment, this overflow-
ing reservoir of manpower is largely wasted.

An important factor in the rise of agricultural production
in developing countries is, in any event, the existing surplus
of unemployed or underemployed workers, by which the
input of farm labor can be enhanced. In the first period of
expansion of productivity, this could be vital, although, in
the course of time, as productivity rises and mechanization
is introduced, a transfer of labor to other lines of production
would be inevitable. In the transition period, however,
everything may turn on the interchangeability of labor with
land, and, in the subsequent stage, of capital and skill with
land and labor. Labor is in oversupply in the developing
countries and is thus the most plentiful ingredient of production, a temporary advantage that ought to hasten the
agricultural revolution there within the next decade. This
situation of labor surplus will be aggravated in the next

decade because of the age structure of the population in developing countries.

When, as it must, transition starts from farming to other branches, the obvious avenues of employment are in the production of manufactured and semimanufactured products and services. This was how the high standards of living in the developed world were achieved.

In low-income countries, agriculture employs some 60 to 70 per cent of the population. As productivity goes up, that percentage goes down, and fewer farmers produce more foodstuffs. Higher incomes diversify the peoples' needs, the demand is larger for industrial commodities and services in a market economy where the pattern of consumption is determined by consumers' choice. Income per head is closely linked with agriculture's diminishing share in employment and in the GNP.

This shift from primary to secondary and tertiary stages of production is already in progress, as witness the smaller share of agricultural output in the total GNP of developing nations—namely, a drop from 35.7 per cent in the period 1950–54 to 30.5 per cent in the years 1960–64.

This shift could raise the standard of living and do away with rural unemployment and underemployment, provided that the process of industrialization follows suit and keeps pace with the fall in the percentage of the population working on the land. It is true that, as a rule, predominantly agricultural countries are poor and that those that industrialize rapidly elevate their standards of living, a process that redounds to their profit and swells the supply of agricultural labor for newly established manufactures. If this occupational changeover comes in the wake of rising agricultural productivity and is due to it, then it also conduces to internal capital formation, it provides, through agricultural exports, a part of the foreign exchange needed for development of industry, and it expands the market for the products of that development.

Industry is expanding quite rapidly in developing countries. From 1960 to 1965, the imports of manufactures by OECD countries from them rose from $1.4 million to $2.9 billion and, over the years 1956–65, by more than threefold. It is, however, proper to add that most of the imports came from a few countries of exceptionally swift progress in industrialization. In the years 1948–64, the progress of industrialization in the developing countries was reflected first in the rate of growth of manufacturing production, which was 7 per cent throughout the period, as against an average of 5 per cent in the developed countries, and, secondly, in the larger share of developing nations in the industrial output of the world—namely, a rise from 5.1 per cent in 1948 to 6.6 per cent in the period 1960–64—and a larger share of industrial production in the total exports of underdeveloped nations—namely, a rise from 11.7 per cent in 1950 to 18 per cent in 1965. This fact is particularly striking when we consider how far the growth of the total exports of developing countries lags behind the general expansion of export trade in the world, a lag due to a falling world demand for primary products. The spread of synthetic materials and the relative drop in the share of food consumption in the total consumption of developed countries are mainly responsible for this trend. Thus, the economies of developing countries display an inclination to align their pattern to that of the developed world:

> The second conclusion to draw, therefore, is that only through a continued, rather rapid movement of people from agriculture into other economic sectors can a more satisfactory development be obtained. A reduction of the wide income gap between agriculture and other activities presupposes such a movement which, consequently, is likely to be the one factor that more than anything else will make it possible eventually to reduce and absorb underemployment in agriculture.

What are, by comparison, the prospects for industry in the developing countries?

In industry land is of minor importance. The relative shortage of land that hampers agricultural expansion in many developing countries does not raise serious problems for industry.

Labour, capital and knowledge are the decisive factors of production. As for agriculture it is also important to consider the general environment in which industry has to work.

Concerning the quantity of labour, the developing countries have a comparative advantage over the developed ones. The very large and growing agricultural population represents an enormous reservoir from which manpower can flow into an expanding industry. By comparison the reservoir of agricultural manpower is now rather small in most developed countries and it is decreasing every year. In some of the older industrial countries it is not far from being exhausted. A large part of the remaining agricultural population consists of elderly people. The large and increasing unemployed population in many developing countries also represents a reservoir which has virtually no counterpart in the developed countries. . . . Industry has three important advantages over agriculture:

1. Modern techniques can as a rule be applied with much less modification (i.e. adaptation to various climates and soils, etc.).

2. It is sufficient that a few managers and technicians have thorough knowledge of these techniques whereas in agriculture many millions of farmers in remote villages need at least some instruction.

3. Industry is usually concentrated in towns and cities where the necessary infrastructure can be provided for without too much difficulty.

The wide income gap between agriculture and the rest of the economy is to a large extent due to the fact that labour productivity is higher in industry than in agriculture. For the reasons mentioned above this is likely to remain so for a very long time to come. Therefore, though more emphasis should be put on the improvement of agriculture in the immediate future, the long-term prospects for development will depend mainly on the process of industrialisation. As it has been in the presently developed countries expansion of industry is likely to become the most important factor of development, once the initial obstacles have been overcome.[26]

26 *The Food Problem of Developing Countries*, pp. 40–42.

There is evident profit in this shift to a secondary stage of production, in as much as "agriculture in the developing countries employs nearly two-thirds of the population but its share of the gross national product is less than one-third. Production per man in agriculture is therefore only one-fourth of what it is on the average in other activities.[27]

It should not be difficult to industrialize the underdeveloped world, seeing that the tendency of industry toward decentralization and its now increasing independence of local raw materials and of nature have been the outstanding feature of global industrial development and should create the conditions that are necesary for the same transformation in the underdeveloped world. In the past, industry inclined to concentrate in specially favored areas: "The existence of a large market and of transport, banking and commercial facilities, as well as the convenience of proximity to related and subsidiary forms of production, abundant supplies of skilled labour and technical knowledge, and saving of time and interest charges"[28]—all these advantages attracted new industry to regions where large-scale industrial organization already existed. But technical progress always tends to undermine these established positions. The new and simplified processes

[27] *Ibid.*, p. 69.

[28] League of Nations, *World Economic Survey, 1931–32,* pp. 18, 19, 20: The spread of the Industrial Revolution is described and explained as follows: "A second factor which has an important bearing on the location of industry is the cost of transport. . . . Transport costs, and especially sea freights, being lower, are a less important factor in the localisation of industries, which are therefore attracted by other forces such as increasing consumers' demand. . . . A further consequence of the reduced costs of sea transport has been the diminished importance of coal deposits, which, in the nineteenth century, were perhaps the dominating factor in the localisation of industries. . . . Not only is it now cheaper to transport coal, but the importance of coal as a source of power constantly diminished.

There have been great improvements in the utilisation and economy of coal and, in addition, competitive sources of power, particularly petroleum and electricity, have been rapidly developed. . . . It is not surprising to find, therefore, a distinct tendency for industry to be released from its former dependence upon proximity to coal supplies so that it is freer to establish itself close to the growing consumers' demand or to sources of bulky raw materials."

are easily emulated in new countries, and displacements in the centers of consumers' demand provide an impetus for the establishment of new industries in new areas.

The development of transport and the rising margin of costs between raw materials and the finished product in relation to the price of raw materials quickened the process of liberation from local "dependencies" and added to the weight of politico-economic factors, such as tariffs and marketing facilities in determining the siting of factories.

Industry, then, is no longer a highly localized activity concentrated in a few choice spots on the earth's surface. The growing simplification of manufacture has enabled many countries to develop industries of their own. The largest rises in industrial output of recent years were in agrarian and not in industrial countries, pointing to a very wide territorial spread. This movement of decentralization is described by J. G. Smith of Birmingham University:

> Scientific progress and technological invention which used to lend support to a free trade policy are now among the most powerful of forces encouraging economic nationalism. Standardisation of processes and output, development of intricate machine tools which can be operated by comparatively unskilled labour after a brief period of training, wide distribution of electrical power and the growth of technical education in every branch of industry, enable new factories to be set up with equal prospects of success almost anywhere throughout the world.[29]

Consequently, industry concentrates, in ever larger measure, in areas unendowed by nature with abundant raw materials. Countries like Belgium, which apart from coal, is almost completely dependent on imported raw materials.[30] Switzerland, with the second highest proportion of industrial

[29] J. G. Smith, "Economic Nationalism and International Trade," *The Economic Journal* (December, 1935), p. 624.

[30] "Belgium Under the Wehrmacht," *The Economist,* Vol. CXL (May 1, 1943), p. 555: "Before the war, there was even an import surplus in coal and coke. . . . Belgium's greatest single industry, the textile industry, entirely depended on imported raw materials."

population in the world—namely 44.9 per cent, in spite of its lack of important raw materials—Italy, South America, Australia, New Zealand, and certain countries in Asia, are cases in point.[31]

Hong Kong is the most extreme example of a country virtually devoid of natural resources, which has even to import a substantial part of its food and water, has a very limited home market, and must ship at least 80 per cent of its manufactures. In spite of this, its industrial growth in the last few years was twice the world rate, averaging 15 per cent per annum. Its industrial exports per head were several times larger than those of Japan. It has swung from the traditional cotton industry to typical growth industries. The facts are phenomenal. In the years 1961 to 1967, output in most of its industries multiplied almost incredibly, yet with minimal supplement of the labor force, and economies of scale are the basis of many of them. The quality of its goods is higher. Capital formation and accumulation have been rapid; acquisition of manufacturing skills is remarkable.

The industrial development of Israel is also exemplary. A country unendowed with natural resources has raised its industrial production since 1950 elevenfold, its industrial labor force by 230 per cent, from 89,000 to 204,000, and its industrial exports rose from $20.3 million to $384 million. Again it can be seen how in industry and local natural resources are becoming interchangeable with capital, skill, and knowledge and with deliberate policies of industrialization.[32]

[31] Clark, p. 183: "In the case of secondary production some unexpected features are also brought to light. The most industrialized country, in the sense of the country where the highest proportion of the population is engaged in secondary production, is Belgium, with 47.8 per cent, followed by Switzerland with 44.9 per cent."

[32] H. Fraenkel, "Industrialisation of Agricultural Countries and the Possibilities of a New International Division of Labour," *The Economic Journal* (June–September, 1943), p. 194: "Production requires plant, raw material and labour (including technical managerial skill), and it is the educational level and the occupational structure of the population which are the most important factors (plant depends on labour, and the synthetic production of an increasing number of raw materials is nowadays possible, and depends in turn on the knowledge and inventiveness of the population)."

To materialize it entails a simultaneous approach on a broad front to agriculture, industry, and services. If there is failure in synchronized action to raise agricultural productivity and to industrialize, large-scale unemployment will result and effective demand not be forthcoming.

Formation of capital could never suffice to meet these requirements, and thus an enormous transfer of capital is the first prerequisite. Again, if domestic markets do not expand, there will not be enough effective demand to ensure the technical and economic minima for the establishment of industrial enterprises and for making possible economies of scale. The rise of consumption is also essential to provide for the efficiency and health of the industrial labor force in its inaugural period.

Availability of natural resources is not a factor restrictive of industrial development in the underdeveloped world. What it is short of are mobile resources such as capital and skill. If the synchronized rise in farm productivity, the freeing of labor from the primary stage of production, and the expansion of the manufacturing industries and services are successful, then the presently unemployed or underemployed reserve of labor in the underdeveloped world could be slotted into the process of global production, as happened with the reserve of labor freed from agriculture in the eighteenth and nineteenth centuries in a number of countries of Europe, when the process of diversification and industrialization absorbed it in what are today developed states. The problem is to equip the surplus population of the underdeveloped world with capital goods, to raise its productivity, and to help it to catch up in economic growth, with limited demographic proliferation and, at the same time, improve its standards of living. It is a problem of reversing the present dynamics, which breed stagnation and widen the gap between developed and underdeveloped countries. The solvents are the agricultural reevolution, occupational reshuffle, industrialization, expansion of effective demand, combined transfer of capital and skill, and access for the wares of the undeveloped countries to the markets of the developed countries.

However, the economic making-over of the underdeveloped countries cannot be confined to raising agricultural productivity, diversification, and industrialization, with the educational training schemes, the acquisition of skilled personnel from abroad, and the large-scale import and investment of capital that those imply. Measures of social and economic policy must precede it, and a reversal of the present trend toward social polarization is an important element of that policy. The excessive income gap between the different classes of the population is a serious handicap to all development efforts, heightens social and political tensions, hampers attempts to better health and efficiency and, certainly not least, to spread knowledge and education.

A socially unwarrantable distribution in incomes cannot be altered radically in the underdeveloped nations overnight. Higher profitability is one of the few incentives and attractions of investment, local or foreign, under conditions of instability and political risk in countries in the throes of internal crises and only on the threshold of their development. Still, an excessive income gap does not favor economic growth. Moreover, accumulation of capital in the hands of a small section of the population not only sharpens social contrasts and tensions but often sets off an export of capital and a flow of funds from underdeveloped to developed countries. This, of course, stultifies the economic objective of putting at the disposal of the underdeveloped countries mobile resources that might galvanize inert factors of production into rigorous life. In these circumstances, a reform of land tenure, a more progressive system of taxation, a more equitable distribution of incomes, extension of social services, and some assimilation of the social structure to the model of the modern welfare state so successfully developed in the West are essential as a framework within which the more basic economic processes of growth and rising productivity, and shifts from primary to secondary and tertiary stages of production can be brought about. By slowing down the export of capital, these internal changes would augment the resources at the disposal of the economies of the underdeveloped world and make for a sounder utilization of such capital as becomes available for purposes of development. All this reforming and transforming in the socio-economic realm involves political and state action. But this does not take away from its importance, its veritable indispensability, in carrying out economic policies and plans that aim at revolutionizing the economies of underdeveloped countries.

The scope of state activity and interference in the economic development of those countries must, by force of circumstances, be wider, more far-reaching, than in developed countries. It cannot be straitjacketed to the measures of social and economic policy hinted at here. Considering the limited entrepreneurial sector, the state's economic initiative and the influence of government action within the underdeveloped economies are imperative if economic growth is to go forward speedily even in periods when entrepreneurs are somewhat lethargic. Government and state activity in the economy would extend in two directions—creation of a framework of administrative, economic, and social reform; straightforward promotion of economic enterprise and investment.

Needless to say, international action is indispensable in the discharge of this policy. The vast economic expansion of our century, advance technology, and the development of new media of communication and transport overpass all national frontiers. The solution of worldwide economic problems— the disparity between the underdeveloped two-thirds of mankind and the highly developed third is most certainly one, and the financing of international trade is another—becomes feasible only within an ambit of worldwide cooperation and integration.

The economic fragmentation of today enlarges and deepens the gap between the several parts of civilization and inflames international tension. The alternative of peace or war is to no inconsiderable extent involved in the contemporary dilemma: global economic integration or confrontation.

The transformation in the underdeveloped countries must be fitted into new departures and endeavors in the developed world, and the drift of that world toward disengagement must be arrested. It all hinges on a new international division of labor, the transfer and mobility of resources, and occupational rearrangement as targets of economic policy.

Conclusions

The abolition of poverty on a global scale is a distinct possibility at the present stage of progress of technology and economics. As George D. Woods, former President of the World Bank, stated:

> We know from our experience—and what I am suggesting is that you proclaim that knowledge—that there is virtually no country, however poor, which cannot achieve and maintain significantly better standards of life for its citizens given reasonable internal political stability and reasonable external support over a period of time.[1]

The prelude to abolition of poverty is a rise in the GNP of the world on an immense scale. This can materialize only if the huge masses in the underdeveloped countries, presently unemployed or underemployed and whose productivity as far as they share in the processes of production is very low, are drawn into the orbit of modern production on a high technological level. This awakening of dormant factors of production is the most successful means of raising the global GNP as the first step toward achieving our end.

Abolition of poverty, in this context, is taken as a pragmatic and empirical concept, shaped by social conscience, the attainable level of economic activity, and the distance from the background of present conditions.

[1] George D. Woods, "10th Conference Highlights: The Development Business Is in Trouble," *International Development Review* (June, 1963).

In the developed countries, rise in the GNP is rapid and underutilized capacity of production, presently, not particularly high. The welfare state and redistributive systems of taxation narrow the gap between social classes so that poverty, as conceived in the developed world, is a phenomenon affecting only limited sections of the population. These pockets of poverty are contracting and should dwindle into insignificance with the expected rise in the GNP at the present rate, coupled with further progress in redistributive measures, while the idea of a subsistence minimum is being expounded at the same time.

In these countries, the average annual rate of growth per capita of the GNP is 3.6 per cent. This increment comes on top of an annual GNP ranging from $450 to $4,000 per capita, compared with $50 to $300 in the developing countries. It is no wonder, therefore, that the projections for the future envisage a standard of living in which poverty would be virtually nonexistent. The developed countries add seven times as much to the income per capita of their population each year as the underdeveloped ones do. Moreover, the political power of the working classes and the economic power of trade unions, the awakening of the social conscience in modern democracies, the progress of income distribution measures, the diffusion of wealth, the spread of social services, old-age insurance, medical care, free education, and, last but not least, the policy of full employment raise and reinforce the ceiling above the poverty line. Although pockets of poverty, slums, and underprivileged minorities still betray symptoms of the pain and suffering inflicted on strata of the population below the poverty line, the sharp edge of poverty is being constantly blunted by the impact of economic growth and income redistribution.

The polarization of modern society is now held in check by constricting blades of the scissors of economic and technological progress and social redistribution of incomes. As that pressure mounts, poverty may become a marginal phenomenon of the modern developed society and, in the course of time, vanish altogether. But poverty cannot be eliminated completely in the developed countries except by the introduction of a minimum income guarantee, which, although it would demand the allocation of a substantial proportion of the national income, is already possible today and becomes more practical from year to year. Besides, the suggested transformation of the economies of the underdeveloped world would, simultaneously, encourage a swifter rise in incomes in the developed world, predicated, as it is, on a shift of its industry to high-income-yielding production of capital goods.

In the underdeveloped world, the manpower surplus is the main problem and perpetuates the low standards of living. Inferior productivity in agriculture and rural unemployment and underemployment heavily oppress the economic conditions of that world, in which 60–70 per cent of the population still works on the land. The rise in farm productivity, through this application of modern agro-science, more irrigation, the use of fertilizers, and the introduction of new crop varieties, would lift the per capita income of the rural population, safeguard a greater self-sufficiency in food, favorably redress the balance of payments, improve nutritional standards, and, finally, free an enormous pool of manpower, as a result, among other causes, of the mechanization of farming. This pool, supplemented by a rural population that is unemployed and underemployed at present, could be a basis for large-scale industrialization and, with rising incomes, prompt the emergence of a more numerous population engaged in the tertiary stage of production—that is, in services.

At the outset, the new industries would have to concentrate mainly on production of consumer goods for the population of the underdeveloped world, with its rising standards of living, and for the population of the developed world to be engaged chiefly in production of capital goods and in sophisticated industries, both still inaccessible to the un-skilled peoples of the underdeveloped world. The change would entail a flow of mobile resources, presently available in the developed world, to the underdeveloped world, im-parting to it skills and technology of modern economic ac-tivity. It would also entail an immense flow of capital from the capital markets and budgets of the developed world, in-cluding the use of newly created liquidity for that purpose.

Abolishing poverty would, therefore, mean first and fore-most a fuller utilization of the now idle factors of produc-tion in the underdeveloped world, primarily manpower that is unemployed or is producing at a low level of productivity, together with a shift of the industrialized countries to capital goods production and sophisticated industries and a further step in the process of redistribution of income and the guar-antee of a minimum income in the developed world.

While a further rise in production in the developed world is conditioned by limitations of manpower and by the need for some underutilization of productive capacity to prevent inflation and there is a surplus of manpower in the under-developed world and while natural resources are diminishing in importance and mobile resources such as capital and skill are becoming more important in modern production, a structural and occupational reshuffle in the underdeveloped nations would go far toward forming a new pattern of global economy.

The strategy of economic development in the two direc-tions—rapid expansion of farming and food production and industrialization of the economies of the developing world—is contingent on a global economic policy of encouragement. The integrated approach to agricultural development and industrialization depends on the provision of capital and skill, on the combination of economic and technological ad-vances. The scope and quality of investment are the keys to economic growth and development and will determine what the gross national product and the level of incomes of the developing countries are to be some years ahead. The expansion of investment, without which the process of abolition of poverty cannot start, and the trend of the 1950's of a more abundant flow of capital to the underdeveloped countries, have been reversed in the 1960's.

The tragedy of the contemporary world is that it is caught in the vortex of two cross-currents: one—deterioration or stagnation that marks some parts of the underdeveloped world; the other—overheated activity and unprecedented prosperity, inflation, and tight capital markets in much of the developed world. Prospects are, if anything, more alarming. The accepted notion that the developing world is catching up with the headstart of the developed world loses all factuality.

The spectacle of a glaring disparity between developed and underdeveloped economies speaks more convincingly than any other argument or exposition of the case for encouraging the economic growth of underdeveloped countries by large-scale investment and influx of capital. It is surely a paradox that the rate of investment is so high in states with overheated economies, shortages of workers, bottlenecks in productive capacity, and inflationary trends, yet so low where so much productive capacity is unused—in particular, the manpower left high and dry in the aftermath of rural unemployment or underemployment and because of unexploited natural resources. The order of priorities is inverted, and the underdeveloped nations are trapped within pincers—one of its jaws economic crisis and famine, the other revolution and war.

The Development Decade, which ought to have found a remedy for this lamentable state of things, is bogged down in shortsightedness of outlook and in the rigid routines of a world that will not discharge its international responsibility. Frustration, futility, and failure are the undertones of the temperate and restrained understatement of the Secretary-General of the United Nations, U Thant, in his letter of congratulations to the President of the World Bank on the occasion of its twentieth anniversary:

> The last annual report of the World Bank has shown that international assistance is falling behind the absorptive capacity of the developing countries, yet it cannot be argued that they have done little to mobilize their domestic resources in the past years. The insufficiency of external aid remains, and the modest target set by the General Assembly in 1961, that the flow of the development capital should represent one per cent of the aggregate national income of developed countries, is far from being reached. Should this situation become worse, as it threatens to do, the growth of developing countries will be seriously retarded.

On another occasion, the Secretary-General emphasized that "unless the world community is prepared to give a massive new impetus to development, it is unlikely that the objectives of the Development Decade will be achieved by 1970" and that the developed countries' contribution will often be the factor that "will tip the scales between stagnation and growth, between increasing poverty and economic progress."

There is consensus as to the laggardness in attaining the objective of the Development Decade. The political and human aspects of this disheartening inadequacy are generally admitted. It is enough to mention the alarm that the Development Decade may become the Decade of Disappointment.

No wonder that, things being so, economic growth is arrested and a spirit of despair and despondency is abroad in the realm of economic aid. Moreover, psychological conditions are worsening to an even grimmer extent. Unwarranted pessimism about the capability of the underdeveloped countries to achieve swift economic progress is being diffused. Notwithstanding that four-fifths of their investment funds originate from local capital formation and not from capital transfers, the approach to exporting capital to them is still largely pedestrian.

Most important of all, the proportion which aid to the underdeveloped world represents of the GNP of the developed world is shrinking even further, considering that the said GNP, which now exceeds $1,850 billion, went up in the last five years at the annual rate of 4 to 5 per cent, but the total of aid was unchanged. Investment in the developed parts of the world is very high, per capita investment in the underdeveloped world is nine times less, in spite of overheated economic activity and inflationary danger in the West. This investment discrepancy is bound to enlarge the already horrifying economic chasm between two-thirds of humanity and one-third of it. The most superficial acquaintance with the facts will bear out the contention that this is not the consequence of any economic weakness in the developed world, affecting its capacity to meet the current emergency and its momentous challenge.

The sense of frustration is deepened by reflection on the moral and intellectual motivations that exist for transferring resources from the developed to the underdeveloped countries with the object of redistributing them on a global scale and reorganizing the world's economy, by the demonstrative effect of high standards of living in the West, and by a comparison with the scope of the Marshall Plan in relation to its purposes. It seems that there is a cycle in the way that developed nations respond to global events. After the First World War, there was a feeling of exuberance and enthusiasm for the New World, for the League of Nations, for world peace and world prosperity. But the tide of soaring optimism ebbed swiftly, and its waves dribbled away into the mire of interwar depression. After the Second World War, the United Nations was set up, and in Bretton Woods the World Bank and IMF were founded. There was an expansion without precedent of aid from the prosperous nations to regions devastated in the fighting, culminating in the Marshall Plan, which involved capital movements of nearly $14 billion from a single country over a three-year period, 80 per cent of it in outright grants and a swelling volume of succor to the under-developed countries ensued—all that against the background of world economy exhausted by the exertions and expenditures of long-drawn-out hostilities.

Since the beginning of the 1960's, the affluent society has been shedding its liabilities more and more. The facts that face us, the trends that prevail, as reflected in the utterance of responsible statesmen, and today's reality are a crushing indictment of developed mankind. The sum of capital transferred from the developed third to the underdeveloped two-thirds of humanity is being whittled down by less satisfactory terms of trade and, if calculated, as it should be, per capita, by the population explosion. Relatively, the decline is even more pronounced, for the net flow of capital is slightly more than one-half of 1 per cent of the GNP of $1,850 billion from a rapidly growing volume of production in the developed third. At the present rate of flow of capital, as a falling share of the swiftly rising GNP in the developed world, any approach to a more acceptable economic relationship between the two divisions of mankind would take hundreds of years to finalize.

Investment in the underdeveloped world is only one instrument of its economic transformation. Transition to a modern economy and society involves a manifold process of change in demographic, cultural, educational, and technological facets, new trade patterns and application of new economic policies. The social gap between classes in the underdeveloped world is certainly a factor retarding development. It affects efficiency, the spirit of cooperation, and training in modern methods of production. At the same time, there is reluctance to invest and little of the entrepreneurial thinking and gusto in the upper classes of society.

The resulting flight of capital, accumulated afterward in highly developed countries, deprives the underdeveloped ones of badly needed assets. The system of taxation does not syphon off enough profits to investment. In these respects, the underdeveloped countries are faced with a dilemma and a contradiction: on the one hand, higher profitability in them is necessary to attract capital; on the other, it aggravates social tensions and does not permit a sufficient expansion of the domestic market.

These are only some of the perplexities that confront the developing world. They should not be interpreted as proof of any failure of economic development or of capital aid and flow to it. In all these areas, progress is swift and astonishing. The gross rate of growth is not less than that of the highly developed world, and the low per capita ratio is due to rapid demographic expansion. A number of developing countries have succeeded in reaching the point of self-sustaining growth, a fact attesting to the truth of the claim that, in the long run, if the underdeveloped world is furnished with the mobile resources of capital and skill, its underdeveloped populations can be harnessed to modern production and modern technology and so enrich all nations to an extent unparallelled in man's records that would, within a measurable period, guarantee the abolition of poverty everywhere on earth.

As the Development Decade draws to its end, a mood of frustration, despair, and dejection threatens to wreck the sober achievements of development and aid and to thwart the initiative and narrow the range of economic progress. On the face of things, the inadequate, almost stagnant, flow of capital to the underdeveloped countries, the agonizingly laggard pace of economic growth per head of their populations, the heavier burden of debt repayments, principal and interest, which, as time goes on, is bound to balance the influx of capital, the population explosion, which devours the lion's share of the increment of the GNP, all point to the futility and defeat of the development effort.

The domestic, economic, and social policies of the developing countries and the performance of their economies seem to be even more discouraging. Inequitable systems of taxation and obsolete laws of land tenure, inflationary financial policies and currency manipulations, corruption and inefficient bureaucracies, the voluminous flight of capital to developed countries, addiction to spectacular but uneconomic prestige projects, misallocation of resources—all these faults reflect immature attitudes and fruitless approaches to the economic and human problems of development.

These, to be sure, are failures and shortcomings, but they are not the whole truth. The immense possibilities of change and transformation manifest themselves in general trends and tendencies and in the actual attainment of a few developing countries. To project the rates of growth and the exploits of that select few onto the whole vast agglomeration of underdeveloped humanity should be the paramount aim of all development policies today.

Excluding the oil-producers, whose swifter growth is due to extensive exploitation of their wells, the following developing countries reached a GNP rate of growth in 1966 exceeding, on the average, 7 per cent: Greece, Hong Kong, Israel, Jordan, Korea, Lebanon, Nicaragua, Panama, Spain, Syria, Taiwan, Thailand, and Yugoslavia. A rate of 5 to 7 per cent was achieved by sixteen others. Even with a high rate of natural increase, such GNP rises are not without substance and meaning in social and human terms. However, it must be borne in mind that, although a rate of growth of 7 per cent or better was recorded in countries that altogether represent less than 15 per cent of the populations of the underdeveloped world, nevertheless these nations are a precept and an example, and the significance of their achievement is incalculable.

The level of food production was stationary in the years 1957–59 and had fallen to an index level of 98 (1957–59 = 100) from the beginning of the 1960's. But in 1967 the index rose by 6 per cent, exceeding the rate of population rise, not only because of favorable weather conditions but also as a result of technological progress and particularly the introduction of new varieties of wheat, rice, and sorghum. The use of fertilizers in the countries in question rose threefold, from 2.3 million tons in 1955–56 to 7 million tons in 1965–66. The doubling and trebling of harvests evoked an unexpectedly vigorous response from the farmers, who grasped this opportunity of improving their lot.

Exports of the manufactures of some developing countries went up prodigiously in 1967: in Hong Kong, by 15 per cent; in Israel, by 11 per cent (and in 1968 by 13 per cent); in Taiwan, by 18 per cent; and in South Korea, by 28 per cent. Four-fifths of the resources invested in the underdeveloped world has originated in local capital formation.

In our age, where human qualities matter most and natural resources are of diminishing importance as ingredients of economic growth, the educational progress of the populations of the developing countries must come first. School attendance there has risen by 12 per cent per annum, several times surpassing the growth of population. This improvement is bound to reinforce what is now termed the "performance drive." In the period 1960–65, the number of literates increased from 879 million to 1,141 million. Technical assistance rose by 50 per cent in the last quinquennium. How much this signifies may be gauged from the fact that, according to the Latin American study of T. W. Schultz, 62 per cent of the additional output in agricultural production in Argentina between 1912 and 1949 was accounted for by residual factors other than the ordinary inputs, and education was the chief residual factor. In Brazil, the equivalent percentage was 45; in Mexico, it was 50.

Thus, in a limited, but experimentally not negligible, area, the agricultural breakthrough, the rate of capital formation, the growth of industrial exports, the impressive educational record, and, first and foremost, the rise of the GNP per capita bear witness to the wide possibilities—and the missed chances—of augmenting production, accelerating economic growth, and raising the standards of life of underdeveloped mankind.

In all these indicators of progress, one factor to be taken into consideration is the lag of the rise of national income behind the structural economic and social changes conducive to it. The profound transformation to be wrought in the economic and social pattern of developing countries before they reach the stage of self-sustaining economic growth and consequently a higher standard of living is a complicated process, which cannot be gauged or evaluated in statistical categories and data alone. The total picture is one of light and shadow, and it seems that despondency, doubt, and desperation are a result not of inexorable conditions or of inherent inadequacies but of failings and shortcomings, of the absence of a political will to shape a new and better world, of ignorance and antiquated thinking. The occasional sparks of luminescence, the islands of success and progress, are abundant testimony of the truth of this conclusion. Political will in underdeveloped countries and the profound change in the totality of economic and social attitudes and patterns of society, as well as basic motivations in those countries, could therefore become instrumental in determining the design of things to come.

Such changes cannot be restricted to the underdeveloped world. What is involved is a new economic departure, which will draw into the process of global economic growth factors of production that are presently dormant, so that there may be more rational and extensive utilization of labor potential and other resources. The conclusion presupposes a no less seismic change in the economic structure of the developed world, promoting and accelerating a second industrial revolution, which could turn the developed world into a vast factory of capital goods. Such advances and adjustments would ultimately herald the abolition of poverty in the developed world, by the speeding up of economic growth and of a shift to high-income branches of economy, with a minimum income assured for all. They would elevate incomes in the underdeveloped world far above the poverty line and well beyond the subsistence levels that presently prevail in the poorest sections of its population.

Following is a listing of the measures of policy designed to bring about the desired consummation:

1. Population control in the underdeveloped world.

2. The raising of agricultural productivity through application of modern agricultural methods, mechanization, and the injection of capital in replacement of manpower in modern husbandry.

3. Greater self-sufficiency and fuller adequacy in food supply in the underdeveloped world, with a view to improving the balance of payments and bettering health and efficiency.

4. Transition to secondary and tertiary stages of production, through a process of industrialization and of the absorption, in manufacturing and in services, of labor made redundant in consequence of the green revolution in agriculture.

5. Fuller utilization of available labor in the underdeveloped world.

6. Massive transfer of mobile resources, such as capital and skill, from the developed to the underdeveloped world.

7. Improvement in the quality, training, and productivity of labor in the underdeveloped world by education in the process of transition to a technological society.

8. Large-scale investment in the developed world in agriculture, industry, and the infrastructure.

9. Initial financing of a rise in consumption in the underdeveloped world to expand its domestic markets.

10. Corrective measures in the utilization of aid and transferred capital through selectivity of investment, social reforms, reducing polarization in the societies of the underdeveloped world, higher taxation, and restriction of export of capital.

11. In the developed world, perpetuation of the present rate of rise in the GNP, facilitated by countercyclical policies.

12. Expansion of the services and amenities of the welfare state, made possible by the rapid per capita rise in the GNP.

13. Introduction in the developed world of a guaranteed minimum and supplementary income (negative income tax).

14. Elimination of restrictions in the developed world on imports of manufactured goods from the underdeveloped world, reduction of protective tariffs, and the introduction of "unilateral free trade."

15. A shift of production in the developed nations from manufacturing consumer goods to high-income industries producing capital goods and to sophisticated industries requiring high skill and a scientific background.

It is clear that these far-reaching measures of policy aimed at wiping out poverty everywhere on earth, once and for all, must be pursued in international coordination and under a global plan.

At this moment of historical time, a falling-off in terms of trade, the population explosion, and the outbreak of famine are fraught with frightening political implications, for the most important basis for a lasting universal peace is to raise living and educational standards in the underdeveloped world as quickly as that can be done.

There is a correlation between the slump in economic conditions in the underdeveloped world and deceleration of aid that is given and between both these processes and the escalation of international tension and the peril of war. As the President of the World Bank Robert S. McNamara has succinctly put it, "in a modernizing world security is development."

In the last twenty years, no shooting war has occurred in the developed world, while the nations of Asia, Africa, and Latin America are seething with disquiet and are tormented by internal and external collisions that threaten mankind with total conflagration. Well over a dozen wars and revolutions have exploded during that period in Asia, Africa, and Latin America and, in some of those countries, the fires of clash and conflict are still ablaze. Unrest and instability are the direct consequence of despair and despondency. The population explosion, worsening terms of trade, the debt detonation, the specter of famine on the horizons of the developing world—these bar any closure of the gap between one-third and two-thirds of civilization. These depress economic conditions, a depression that hunger, disease, and ignorance follow only too quickly.

The second half of the twentieth century may well prove to be the most momentous epoch in recorded history. It is the first time in the annals of man that modern technology and modern economics provide the means and instruments for the abolition of poverty and, consequently, for the elimination of ignorance and the alleviation of disease. This is not a utopian dream. It is a practical objective within our grasp, a vision that could become a reality.

The gross national product of the developed and underdeveloped parts of the world, taken together, has reached the stupendous sum of over $2,300 billion a year and is rising at the impressive annual rate of over $100 billion. A transformation is taking place in the productivity of modern economy. Automation, computers, and atomic energy are cases in point. In agriculture, the extensive use of fertilizers, the dramatic expansion of irrigated areas, the Indus and Nile projects, and, outstandingly, the introduction of new crop varieties, sometimes doubling and trebling the yield of the soil—these amount to a revolution and open up new vistas for the extinction of hunger and malnutrition.

The great discoveries of gas and oil added vastly to the power resources of the universe. The industrial exports of the underdeveloped to the developed nations more than doubled within a decade, and the possibilities of further industrialization, if, thanks to preferential tariffs, the markets of the developed world become accessible to the underdeveloped nations, are practically boundless. The teeming millions of Asia, Latin America, and Africa, now underemployed, could be drawn into the orbit of modern technological production and multiply the wealth of the world.

New forces are being liberated all over the globe and are changing the image of economy and society.

A new departure, a new economic policy, are imperative, and the propitious conditions for them exist in the high level of technology, the new dimensions in economics, and a rational approach to the new elements of economic and social life, which are the overmastering attributes of our age.

Poverty has been with mankind from time immemorial, but today it appears incongruous against the background of modern economy and society. The dream of its abolition is as old as man, down all the aeons from ancient utopia to twentieth-century socialism. The problem lends itself today to handling by pragmatic methods, and within the confines of a pluralistic democratic society. This is a new departure in the war on poverty, a war that will end in victory if new economic, technological, and social factors are applied in the quest for a society where no one will again be poor.

Bibliography

ABS, HERMANN J.; FRANKS, OLIVER; and SPROUL, ALLAN. "Bankers' Mission to India and Pakistan, February–March, 1960." Letter to Eugene R. Black. International Bank for Reconstruction and Development, Washington, D.C.

ADLER, JOHN H. "The Progress of Economic Development." Talk before Economic Roundtable Session, Fifty-first National Foreign Trade Convention, November 18, 1964, New York. Washington, D.C.: International Bank for Reconstruction and Development.

BANK FOR INTERNATIONAL SETTLEMENTS. *Thirty-eighth Annual Report, April 1, 1967–March 31, 1968.* Basel, Switzerland, June, 1968.

BARACH, ARNOLD B. *The New Europe and Its Economic Future.* New York: Macmillan, 1964.

BLACK, EUGENE R. "Address to the Economic and Social Council of the United Nations." April 24, 1961, New York. Mimeographed.

———. "Some Principles for Development Assistance." Statement at a meeting of the Development Assistance Group, March 9, 1960, Washington, D.C.

BOWLES, CHESTER. "Priority for Human Dignity." *International Development Review,* VII, 3 (September, 1965).

BOWMAN, ISAIAH. *Limits of Land Settlement: A Report on Present-Day Possibilities.* New York: Council on Foreign Relations, 1937.

———. *The Pioneer Fringes.* 1931.

BROWN, FREDERICK. *Statistical Yearbook of the World Power Conference.* No. 1. London: Central Office, World Power Conference, 1933, 1934.

BROWN, LESTER R. "The Agricultural Revolution in Asia." *Foreign Affairs* (July, 1968).

———. "Population Growth, Food Needs, and Production Problems." *World Population and Food Supplies, 1980.* Special Pub. No. 6. Madison, Wis.: American Society of Agronomy, 1965.

———. *Man, Land, and Food: Looking Ahead at World Food Needs.* Foreign Agricultural Economic Report No. 11. Washington, D.C.: Economic Research Service, U.S. Department of Agriculture, November, 1963.

BURNHAM, DONALD C. "Productivity Improvement: A Worldwide Need."

Address at the Fifty-fourth National Foreign Trade Convention, National Foreign Trade Council, October 30, 1967, New York.

BUTLER, HAROLD. *Problems of Industry in the East, with Special Reference to India, French India, Ceylon, Màlaya, and the Netherlands Indies.* Geneva: International Labour Office, 1938.

BUXTON, DOROTHY FRANCES. *The Economics of the Refugee Problem.* Intro. by Norman Angell. London: Focus Publishing Co., 1938.

CARR-SAUNDERS, A. M. *World Population: Past Growth and Present Trends.* Royal Institute for International Affairs. Oxford: Clarendon Press, 1936.

———. "Fallacies About Overpopulation." *Foreign Affairs,* IX, 4 (July, 1931).

——— et al. *The Population Problem: The Experts and the Public.* London: George Allen and Unwin, 1938.

CLARK, COLIN. *The Economics of 1960.* London: Macmillan, 1942.

———. *The Conditions of Economic Progress.* London: Macmillan, 1940.

——— and CRAWFORD, J. G. *The National Income of Australia.* London: Angus and Robertson, 1938.

CLARK, GROVER. *The Balance Sheet of Imperialism: Facts and Figures on Colonies.* 1936.

CLELAND, WENDELL. *The Population Problem in Egypt.* Ephrata, Pa.: Science Press, 1936.

CROCKER, W. R. *The Japanese Population Problem: The Coming Crisis.* London: George Allen and Unwin, 1931.

DITTMAR, HANS. "Ist durch Ertragssteigerung eine Selbstversorgung Europas moeglich?" *Uebersee-Post,* No. 3 (1943).

DODD, STUART CARTER. *Social Relations in the Near East.* Beirut: American University of Beirut, 1940.

———. *Controlled Experiment on Rural Hygiene in Syria.* Beirut: American University of Beirut, 1934.

EEC COMMISSION. "Development of a European Capital Market." November, 1966.

EHRLICH, PAUL. *The Population Bomb.* New York: Ballantine, 1968.

FAO. *The State of Food and Agriculture 1966.* Doc. CL/47/2. Rome, 1966.

FAWCETT, C. B. "Some Factors in Population Density." *Problems of Population.* Edited by G. H. L. F. Pitt Rivers. Report of proceedings, Second General Assembly, International Union for the Scientific Investigations of Population Problems. London, 1931.

FERENCZI, IMRE. "Contre Migration et Politique d'Emigration." *Revue Economique Internationale* (December, 1938).

———. *The Synthetic Optimum of Population.* Paris: League of Nations, 1938.

FISHER, A. G. B. *The Clash of Progress and Security.* New York: Augustus M. Kelley, Publishers, 1935.

FLEMING, J. MARCUS, and LOVASY, GERTRUD. "Fund Policies and Procedures in Relation to Compensatory Financing of Commodity Fluctuations." *IMF Staff Papers,* VIII (November, 1960).

FLEMISH ECONOMIC ASSOCIATION. *Development Aid.* Eighth Scientific Congress of Flemish Economists, May, 1967, Ghent, Belgium.

FREEMAN, ORVILLE L. *World Without Hunger.* New York: Frederick A. Praeger, 1968.

FRIEDMAN, IRVING S. "International Problems of Economic Development." Address to the Canadian Political Science Association, June 7, 1967, Ottawa, Canada.

GALBRAITH, JOHN KENNETH. "A Positive Approach to Economic Aid." *Foreign Affairs,* XXXIX, 3 (April, 1961).

GAUD, WILLIAM S. "Foreign Aid Today: Facts and Fancies." Address before the National Foreign Policy Conference for Education Leaders, U.S. State Department, June 20, 1968, Washington, D.C.

———. "The Green Revolution." *International Development Review* (June, 1968).

GLASS, D. V. *Population Policies and Movements in Europe.* Oxford: Clarendon Press, 1940.

HALL, N. F. *Preliminary Investigation into Measures of a National or International Character for Raising the Standard of Living.* Geneva: Economic Committee, League of Nations, 1938.

HANCOCK, W. K. *Survey of British Commonwealth Affairs.* Vol. II. *Problems of Economic Policy, 1918–1939.* Part I. Royal Institute for International Affairs. London: Humphrey Milford, 1940.

HELLER, WALTER. *New Dimensions of Political Economy.* Cambridge, Mass.: Harvard University Press, 1966.

HEVESY, PAUL DE. *World Wheat Planning and Economic Planning in General.* London: Oxford University Press, 1940.

HICKS, J. R. *Value and Capital.* London: Oxford University Press, 1939.

HIMADEH, S. E. *Economic Organization of Syria.* Beirut: American University of Beirut, 1936.

HOPE-SIMPSON, JOHN. *Refugees.* Preliminary Report of a Survey. Royal Institute for International Affairs. London: Chatham House, 1938.

———. *The Refugee Problem.* Report of a Survey. Royal Institute for International Affairs. London, 1938.

———. "The Work of the Greek Refugee Settlement Commission." Address before the Royal Institute for International Affairs. *Journal of the R.I.I.A.* (November, 1929).

HØST-MADSEN, POUL. "How Much Capital Flight from Developing Countries?" *Finance and Development,* II, 1 (March, 1965).

IBRD. *Annual Report 1966.* Washington, D.C., 1967.

IMF. *Annual Report 1966.* Washington, D.C., 1967.

INSTITUTE OF PACIFIC RELATIONS. *The Peopling of Australia.* Series no. 4. Melbourne, Australia: Melbourne University Press, 1933.

INTERNATIONAL BANK FOR RECONSTRUCTION AND DEVELOPMENT. *Economic*

Growth and External Debt. Vol. II. Staff Study of the Economic Department Report No. EC-122, March 12, 1964.

INTERNATIONAL LABOUR OFFICE. *International Labour Review.* XXXIX, 3 (March, 1939).

JACOBSSON, PER. *International Monetary Problems, 1957–1963: Selected Speeches of Per Jacobsson.* Washington, D.C.: International Monetary Fund, 1964.

———. "The Economic Situation of the Western World." *Skandinaviska Banken,* XXXVII, 3 (July, 1956).

JEROME, H. *Migration and Business Cycles.* New York: National Bureau of Economic Research, 1926.

KANEDA, HIROMITSU. *The Sources and Rates of Productivity Gains in Japanese Agriculture as Compared with the U.S. Experience.* No. 113. Economic Growth Center, Yale University, 1967.

KIMBLE, GEORGE H. T. *The World's Open Spaces.* London: Thomas Nelson and Sons, 1939.

KINDLEBERGER, CHARLES. *Europe's Postwar Growth.* Cambridge, Mass.: Harvard University Press, 1967.

KOPELUK, M. "Syrian Economics Today." *Palestine and Middle East* (Tel-Aviv), IX, 3 (1937).

KUZNETS, S. *Economic Development and Cultural Change.* July, 1960.

LADAS, STEPHAN P. *The Exchange of Minorities: Bulgaria, Greece, and Turkey.* Cambridge, Mass.: Bureau of International Research, Harvard University and Radcliffe College, 1932.

LAMERS, ERNEST. "How Fast Will the Gap Close?" *International Development Review,* IX, 1 (March, 1967).

LEAGUE OF NATIONS. *World Economic Survey, 1938–39.*

MACMILLAN, W. M. *Warning from the West Indies.* London: Penguin, 1938.

McNAMARA, ROBERT S. "Toward the Prevention of Seismic Social Shock." Address given February 24, 1967.

MASON, EDWARD S. *Foreign Aid and Foreign Policy.* New York: Harper & Row, 1964.

MATTHEWS, ALLAN F. "Resources and Norms in Development Planning." *International Development Review,* IX, 2 (June, 1967).

MOMBERT, PAUL. *Grundriss der Sozialekonomik.* Vol. II. *Die natürlichen und technischen Beziehungen der Wirtschaft.* Tübingen: Verlag Mohr, 1914.

OECD. *The Food Problem of Developing Countries.* Paris, 1968.

———. *Aid to Agriculture in Developing Countries.* Paris, 1968.

OECD OBSERVER. "Agricultural Policies: A Twenty-three Nation Survey." No. 25. Paris, December, 1966.

OHLIN, GORAN. *Population Control and Economic Development.* Paris: Development Center, OECD, 1967.

———. *Foreign Aid Policies Reconsidered.* Paris: Development Center, OECD, 1966.

PITT-RIVERS, G. H. L. F. *Problems of Population.* Report of the proceedings, Second General Assembly, International Union for the Scientific Investigation of Population Problems, June 15–18, 1931. London: George Allen and Unwin, 1932.

PREBISCH, RAUL. "Introduction." *International Monetary Issues and the Developing Countries: Report of the Group of Experts,* TD/B/32, TD/B/C. 3/6, November 1, 1965.

PRICE, HARRY BAYARD. *The Marshall Plan and Its Meaning.* Ithaca, N. Y.: Cornell University Press, 1955.

QUARANTA, FERDINANDO. *Ethiopia: An Empire in the Making.* London: P. S. King and Sons, 1939.

REID, ESCOTT. *The Future of the World Bank.* Washington, D. C.: International Bank for Reconstruction and Development, 1965.

———. "Rich Lands, Poor Lands: Recollections and Reflections." *Finance and Development,* II, 1 (March, 1965).

REUTER, EDWARD BYRON. *Population Problems.* Philadelphia: Lippincott, 1923.

ROBOCK, STEFAN. "It's Good for Growth, but Who's Swallowing?" *Columbia University Journal of World Business* (November–December, 1967).

ROYAL ECONOMIC SOCIETY. *The Economic Journal,* London (December, 1935).

SCOTT, JOHN. *Hunger: Must We Starve?* New York: Time, 1966.

SISMONDI, J. C. L. S. DE. *Nouveaux Principes d'Economic Politique,* Vol. II. 2nd ed.

STALEY, EUGENE. *World Economy in Transition.* New York: Council on Foreign Relations, 1939.

———. *Peaceful Change.* Proceedings, Tenth International Studies Conference, June 28–July 3, 1937. Paris: International Institute of Intellectual Cooperation, League of Nations, 1938.

SUMYK, GEORGE B. "The Third Horseman." *Frontier,* XXVII, 2 (Summer, 1966).

SUNDARA RAJAN, K. S. "India's Population Problem." *Finance and Development,* II, 3 (September, 1965).

TAYLOR, GRIFFITH. *Environment, Race, and Migration.* Toronto: University of Toronto Press, 1937.

THOMPSON, WARREN S. *Population Problems.* New York: McGraw-Hill, 1935.

———. *Danger Spots in World Population.* New York: Alfred A. Knopf, 1930.

THORP, WILLARD L. *Development Assistance Efforts and Policies.* Paris: Development Assistance Committee, OECD, 1965.

TITMUSS, RICHARD N. *Poverty and Population: A Factual Study of Contemporary Waste.* London: Macmillan, 1938.

TOYNBEE, ARNOLD. *Population and Food Supply.* McDougall Memorial Lecture. Rome: FAO, 1959.

UNITED NATIONS. *Yearbook of National Accounts Statistics, 1966.* New York, 1967.

———. *Demographic Yearbook 1965.* New York, 1966.

———, CONFERENCE ON TRADE AND DEVELOPMENT. *Toward a New Trade Policy for Development.* Doc. E/Conf. 46/3, February 12, 1964.

———, DEPT. OF ECONOMIC AND SOCIAL AFFAIRS. *The External Financing of Economic Development: International Flow of Long-Term Capital and Official Donations, 1962–1966.* Doc. E/4438, New York, 1968.

———, DEPT. OF ECONOMIC AND SOCIAL AFFAIRS. *The United Nations Development Decade: Proposals for Action.* Doc. E/3613, New York, 1962.

U.S. DEPARTMENT OF AGRICULTURE. *Changes in Agriculture in Twenty-six Developing Nations, 1948–1963.* Foreign Agricultural Economic Report No. 27. Washington, D.C., November, 1965.

U.S. DEPARTMENT OF STATE. *The Scope and Distribution of United States Military and Economic Assistance Programs.* Report to the President of the United States. Washington, D.C.: Committee to Strengthen the Security of the Free World, 1963.

U.S. PRESIDENT'S SCIENCE ADVISORY COMMITTEE. "Report of the World Food Panel." Vol. I. Washington, D.C., June, 1967.

WHITBECK, R. H., and PINCH, V. C. *Economic Geography: A Regional Survey.* New York: McGraw-Hill, 1941.

WOODS, GEORGE D. "Development: The Need for New Directions." Address to the Swedish Bankers Association, October 27, 1967, Stockholm, Sweden.

———. "The Development Decade in the Balance." *Foreign Affairs,* XLIV, 2 (January, 1966).

———. "Address to the Board of Governors." 1965 Annual Meeting, International Bank for Reconstruction and Development, September 27, 1965, Washington, D.C.

———. "Statement to the Ministerial Meeting, Development Assistance Committee, OECD, Paris, July 22, 1965." Washington, D.C.: International Bank for Reconstruction and Development.

———. "Tenth Conference Highlights: The Development Business Is in Trouble." *International Development Review* (June, 1963).

WRIGHT, FERGUS CHALMERS. *Peaceful Change, Population, and Peace.* Paris: International Institution of Intellectual Cooperation, League of Nations, 1939.

WRIGHT, HAROLD. *Population.* Cambridge, Eng.: Cambridge University Press, 1923.

ZIMMERMANN, ERICH W. *World Resources and Industries: An Appraisal of Agricultural and Industrial Resources.* New York: Harper & Row, 1933.

ZISCHA, ANTON. *Italien in der Welt.* Leipzig: Wilhelm Goldman Verlag, 1937.